MW01129705

HIGHER FASTER LONGER
UNSUNG GENIUS: WALLY FUNK

Janet Ivey Duensing & Loretta Hall

Illustrated by Katie Grayson

Janet Ivey Duensing

Keep looking up!

Traitmarker Books
traitmarkerbooks.com
traitmarker@gmail.com

ORDERING BOOKS FOR QUANTITY SALES
Special discounts are available on quantity purchases by corporations, associations, and others. For details, contact the author at the email address above.

ATTRIBUTIONS
Interior Text Font: Minion Pro
Interior Title Fonts: Futura, Silom, and Handwriting 3
Editor: Sharilyn Grayson
Typesetter: Katie Grayson
Cover Design & Interior Illustrations: Katie Grayson

BOOK PUBLISHING INFORMATION
Traitmarker Books
ISBN 978-1-0879-0958-5
Published by TRAITMARKER BOOKS

HIGHER FASTER LONGER
UNSUNG GENIUS: WALLY FUNK
Written by Janet Ivey Duensing and Loretta Hall

Illustrated by Katie Grayson

Dedicated to

The Women of Mercury 13:
Wally Funk
Myrtle Cagle
Jerrie Cobb
Janet Dietrich
Marion Dietrich
Sarah Gorelick
Jane "Janey" Briggs Hart
Jean Hixson
Rhea Woltman
Gene Nora Stumbough
Irene Leverton
Jerri Truhill
Bernice Steadman

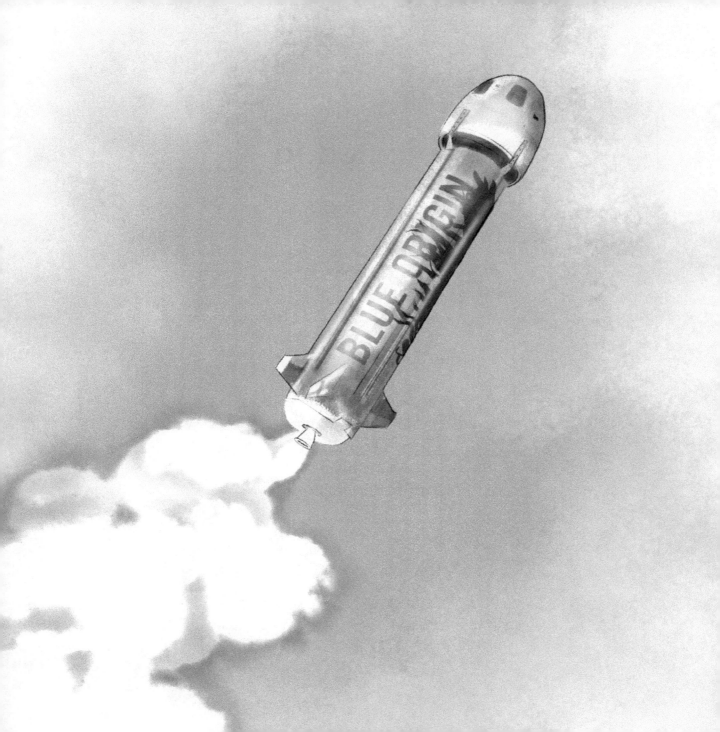

Contents

BEFORE YOU READ...

I got a chance to meet Wally virtually in April of 2020. I had seen the film *Mercury 13* and was mesmerized by the story of these women and truly WOWED by Wally, whose inexhaustible spirit is so incredibly enchanting and inspiring. I had turned my entire business to an online platform when all live performances and camps were canceled and removed from my calendar. I may have sat down and cried in my coffee, but something deep in me spoke to me and said, "Oh for crying out loud…all you need is to be around kids. Take what you have to them!" The Janet's Planet Astronaut Academy was born, and I took Janet's Planet to Zoom and started offering free space and science classes.

A dear friend named Melinda Viteri came online to the Academy and talked about aviation and being a pilot and one of the Ninety-Nines (an international organization of licensed women pilots from 44 countries who LOVE TO FLY!) After her talk, Melinda said, "You know who you need to ask to come on? Wally Funk!" I said, "Do you really think she would be willing to come and talk to the students?"

Melinda, who seems to know everyone on the planet, insisted. Within several days, I was on the phone with Wally, and once again blown away by her zest, her energy for life and flying, and her desire to communicate that love of adventure with all generations!

We had a capacity crowd on our Zoom call that day as Wally amazed us with all that she has done to further aviation and women in space and how she never, ever, EVER, lets up in her intent to be positive and look for the stars.

Over the last few months, we have become pals. She called me one Saturday and said, "I just love the sound of your voice! It really gets me going!" IMAGINE! Me? She in every way was the one that REALLY GOT ME GOING, and with a wonderful collaboration with her memoir author Loretta Hall, Wally agreed to be the next woman in my UNSUNG GENIUS series of books. This Unsung Genius story celebrates a pioneer whose daringness has opened doors for women in aviation and continues to inspire all who hear her story.

Wally Funk's life and indefatigable spirit are testaments to her passion for life, aviation, and all things UP! She is energy, focus, and positivity personified. As self-assured and self-possessed as any human you will ever meet, Wally has incorporated her love of the Taos mountains and all the wisdom that they embody in her hypersonic life. DAUNTLESS, FEARLESS, and INTREPID are just a few words that describe Wally. Wally is spark and spunk, and she walks always with her eyes turned upward.

In these pages, I hope you see that Wally Funk has a smile, a vitality, and a heart as wide as the world itself.

Imagine this…Wally Funk is writing the story of her life celebrating all the things she has done and dreaming of all the things she has yet to do, and in this way, she is writing to her genius self and to the genius in you!

At the end of the book, you'll find space to write to your genius self and jot down all the amazing things you see yourself doing in the future! See the smile and mirth on Wally's face as you read all about this history-making woman cataloging the many milestones and victories of her life. I can pretty much guarantee you that as Wally tells her story, she is simultaneously cheering you on as she encourages you to ALWAYS LOOK UP and HAVE A SUPERSONIC LIFE!

Janet Ivey Duensing | Nashville, Tennessee

LETTER TO GENIUS YOU

Dear Genius You,

How are you, kid? I am pleased as punch that you are sitting down to read my story. I have had a FANTASTIC life, and it just keeps getting better and better! I hope you enjoy reading all about the things that I was able to do and accomplish, and I hope by the time you finish this book, you'll have a better understanding about the "girl who always loved to go higher and faster LONGER!"

For anyone who takes the time to read about me and read this letter, I just want to tell you to be sure and let your GENIUS LIGHT SHINE! Remember this, NEGATIVITY CONTAMINATES ENERGY! It slows you down. Your goal is to keep saying, "Yes, I can do it." And keep moving forward with confidence.

Often I end a speech this way, so I guess I'll close this letter to you this way:

Take a big breath in and breathe out...then read this poem by Nancy Wood:

I am but a footprint on the Earth
A wing against the sky.
A shadow over water
A voice beneath the fire.
I am one footstep going on and on and on.

all the best,

Eileen

Aviator, Adventurer, Astronaut

1

A Toddler and Bolts and a Superman Cape

Dear Genius You,

Once you start reading about me, I think you'll say, "WOW, SHE WAS FEARLESS!" At least, that's what I hope you'll think! I've never once been afraid to go with gusto for something that I wanted to do. All my life, when a good opportunity has come up, I've grabbed it. I hope you grab your good opportunities, too! Settle in, and hang on...who wants to take flight with me? Let me start by telling you how it all happened.

All the best,
Amelia

When I was only two years old, my parents took me to the airport outside my home town. It was a special day, because a big airplane was there. We lived in Taos, a small town in northern New Mexico, and the only planes that were usually at our airport were little ones that could hold one or two people. But that day, a DC-3 was there. It had a fat engine on the front of each wing instead of a small one on its nose, and it could carry more than twenty people.

I don't remember that day, of course. I mean, who does remember when they were two years old? But my mother took a picture of me. I walked right up to that big airplane to get a closer look. I was so short I couldn't really see the whole plane, but I could see one of its front wheels.

The wheel was taller than I was!

I was already a curious child, and I must have wanted to see how such a big machine was put together. I bent over a little so I could look into a metal piece where the wheel was attached to the plane. I reached in and tried to turn the nut that held the wheel on. That was just the start of my fascination with mechanical things, especially airplanes. I guess you could call that picture my first ever pre-flight safety inspection! Haha!

I always felt loved and cared for, and my parents also gave me a lot of freedom. When I would leave the house to ride my horse, Victor, or ride my bike, Mother would say, "If you fall and get hurt, BRUSH YOURSELF OFF AND KEEP GOING! If you break a bone, come home, and we'll see the doctor." Haha! Can you imagine that? How I loved, LOVED, loved, my mother! My parents gave me the great gift of confidence, and I've never had any fears. "No fears in our house," my parents would say. I learned from them that you have to understand how things work, and that way you can use them correctly and not have to be afraid of what might happen. Throughout my career and life, they encouraged me to meet whatever crisis came along with calm determination.

Sometimes Mother would ask me, "Where are you going to sleep tonight?" The answer might be in the barn, in the tree house I had built, outside under the stars, or maybe my very own bedroom. It just all depended on what struck my fancy.

You might also find me hanging out with my Native American friends who were a part of the Taos Pueblo tribe. They were like a second family to me. They taught me how to fish, hunt, camp, and survive in the wilderness. And they taught me a saying that I've used all my life. If something goes wrong and I can't do anything about it, I just say, "THROW IT A FISH" and let it go. I don't know exactly how that particular expression came about.

I imagine it might have referred to getting a hungry animal to stop pestering or threatening you. If you throw it a fish, it will be satisfied and stop bothering you. Can you imagine the first person to discover that throwing a pesky animal a fish actually distracted it and made it go away? Hahaha!

All I know is that expression has always helped me deal with annoying or frustrating events. I enjoy my life, and I don't want to waste time and energy becoming upset or dwelling on issues I can't control. It's better to LET IT GO and just move on. So, the next time something is troubling you, imagine throwing that problem a FISH, and see how you feel! It ALWAYS makes me feel better.

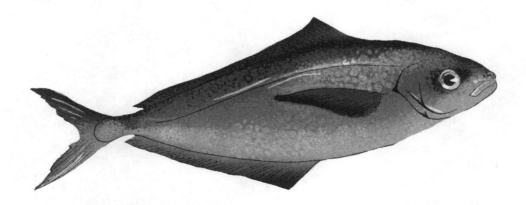

And speaking of things that really know how to let go, just think of birds! Have you ever watched a bird surf the air currents? To birds, the sky is not empty, but a landscape of invisible features — wind gusts, currents of warm rising air, and streams of air pushed upward by ground features such as mountains. Learning to ride air currents allows some birds to travel long distances while minimizing the exertion of beating their wings. A bird who knows how to soar on air currents can stay aloft for hours without flapping its wings. Their movements can teach you a lot about life…will you use the wind gusts as power and thrust and the warm rising air to keep you aloft? Or will you flap your wings to exhaustion? How about you and I be soaring birds, not the flapping kind?

You see, there were lots of birds where I lived. Little ones like sparrows and big ones like eagles. I loved watching them fly freely through the air. I believe that watching the birds fly made me want to fly, too!

When I was five years old, I decided to try to FLY! I put on the Superman costume my parents had given me for Christmas. I figured out our barn would be high enough to fly off and soar! The edge of its roof was so high my daddy couldn't touch it when he stretched up his arm. I knew I might not fly on my very first try. Baby birds fail at this sometimes. So, I spread a pile of hay on the ground next to the barn. I am grateful I had some thought of safety and landing! Then I climbed a ladder and got on the roof. I stood at the edge and spread my arms out, clutching the edges of my cape in my hands. I bent my knees, took a deep breath, and JUMPED OFF THE ROOF, flapping my arms as hard as I could.

WELL, IT WAS A GOOD THING I had spread that hay on the ground! Gravity did its job, and I fell instead of floated into that big mound of hay. WHEE! It was so much fun! I got up and dusted myself off. Then I climbed back up the ladder and tried again. This time, I jumped HIGHER and flapped my cape EVEN HARDER! But I landed in the hay again. WHY COULDN'T I FLY?

Well, first off, my cape wasn't really like the wings that carried birds through the air. And I didn't have a propeller on my nose like an airplane did. I finally had to admit that I couldn't fly without more help. BUT that realization DIDN'T stop me from knowing that I was still meant to FLY!

THE FOUR FORCES OF FLIGHT:

Here is a quiz for you!

What are the four forces of flight?

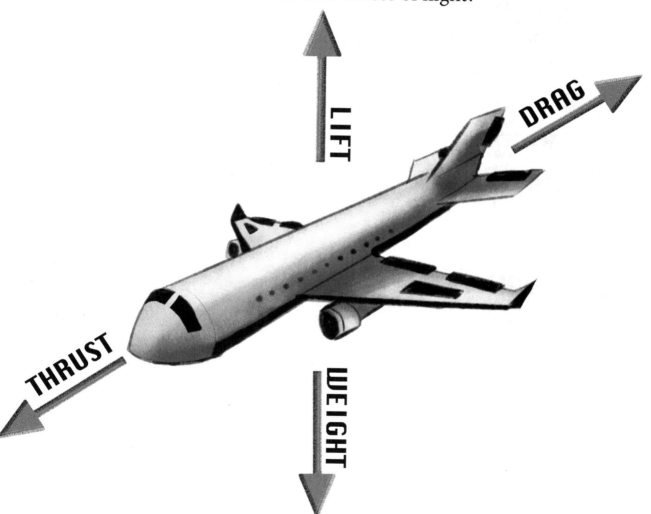

Lift, weight, drag, and thrust! Yes, indeed!

SONIC

Birds and airplanes both have a streamlined body structure, which is necessary for flight.

SUPERSONIC

The body of a plane or aircraft is made of light materials, and birds have light bones and feathers in their bodies.

HYPERSONIC

BIRDS AND AIRCRAFT both have wings (somewhat similar in shape) and use them for flight!

SONIC

Sonic means the speed of sound in air, about 768 miles per hour at sea level. That speed is called Mach 1.

SUPERSONIC

If you go supersonic in an airplane, that means that you are flying speeds from one to five times the speed of sound in air. Supersonic speeds are somewhere between 921 and 3,836 mph.

HYPERSONIC

In aerodynamics, a hypersonic speed is one that greatly exceeds the speed of sound, at speeds of Mach 5 (five times the speed of sound in air) and above. Hypersonic speeds are between 3,836 and 7,673mph. Generally, hypersonic speeds are the point at which the molecules of air that surround the aircraft start to change by breaking apart and/or picking up electrical charge.

2

Taos Mountains

Dear Genius You,

Have you ever donned a cape and pretended you could fly? Do you like to do things that maybe other kids don't? GOOD FOR YOU! BE YOU! Always and forever, follow your own path, and don't let anyone tell you that you can't or shouldn't or won't! Haha! I've been proving people wrong about what women can do all my life... and you can, too! Now settle in, and let me tell you a bit more about where I grew up and the mountain that still to this day speaks to me.

all the best,

30

The village of Taos was a wonderful place to grow up in the 1940s. It was a small town where people cared about each other. When I was in elementary school, I could walk, ride my bicycle, or ride my Palomino pony Victor all over town by myself.

SONIC

Located in the Sangre de Cristo Mountains of New Mexico, the town of Taos takes its name from a word meaning "place of red willows" in the native Taos language.

Taos had been a Native American Pueblo for more than 1,000 years. Native Americans still live in the Pueblo, and Hispanic and Anglo people have been living in the neighboring town since 1795. I liked to go to the Pueblo to play with my friends. I was always a tomboy, and many of my friends were boys. We would go camping, and they showed me how to build a campfire without using matches.

SUPERSONIC

Wally isn't usually a girl's name. When I was little, my full name, Mary Wallace, didn't fit on my Christmas stocking. My grandfather suggested shortening Wallace to Wally. It fit on my stocking, and it FIT ME MUCH BETTER, TOO!

I always loved sleeping outdoors. There was no light pollution when I was a kid. At nighttime where I grew up, the sky was dark, the stars were bright, and the air was thin because we lived at an elevation of 7,000 feet. Boy oh boy, was the night sky full of brilliant stars! No sleeping in a tent for me! I wanted to enjoy that spectacular sky until my eyes couldn't stay open. The Taos mountains and the starry skies are probably the reason I've been fascinated with space and flight all my life.

I grew up in a Christian family, and my religion has always been important to me. I sang in church and went to Sunday school. It is an important part of my spiritual life.

But another part of my spiritual life came from the Taos Pueblo Indian tradition. Taos Mountain is sacred to the Taos Pueblo people. It has a very spiritual quality, too. When I was a child, my mother would tell me to look out my window at that mountain every morning. "Look at it, and it's going to tell you in your heart and in your mind what is expected of you to do today and what you're going to achieve," she would say. And that's what I would do.

Even as an adult, I still love that mountain. When I'm not living in Taos, I hang a picture of Taos Mountain on a wall of my home so I can look at it every day. Its mighty form makes me feel strong and confident.

SONIC

Taos Mountain is in the Sangre de Cristo Mountains, which is part of the Rocky Mountains. It is known locally as Pueblo Peak, and it is 12,305 feet high. Local beliefs attribute power to the Mountain. Many people who have come to settle in Taos and have had successful businesses or relationships there claim that it happened because "the Mountain allowed it."

3

A Girl and Her Planes

Dear Genius You,

Have you ever ridden in a plane? I'll never forget the thrill of the first time I got to sit in the co-pilot seat and experience flight. Most of all, I hope you take every opportunity to pilot your own life in the direction and destination of your choosing!

all the best,

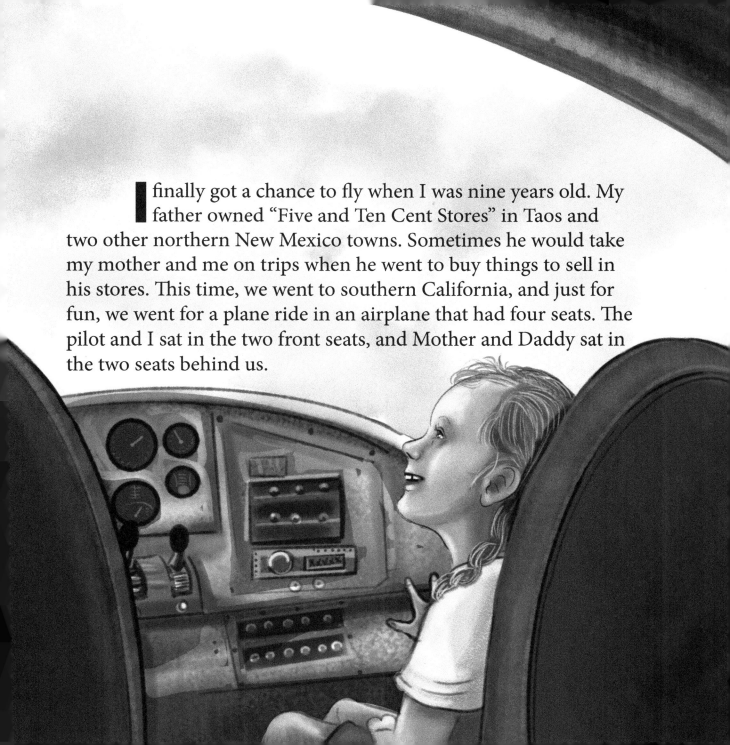

finally got a chance to fly when I was nine years old. My father owned "Five and Ten Cent Stores" in Taos and two other northern New Mexico towns. Sometimes he would take my mother and me on trips when he went to buy things to sell in his stores. This time, we went to southern California, and just for fun, we went for a plane ride in an airplane that had four seats. The pilot and I sat in the two front seats, and Mother and Daddy sat in the two seats behind us.

When we took off, I could feel my body being pushed back into the seat as the plane left the ground and flew faster. I watched needles move in all the gauges that told us how fast we were flying, which direction we were going, and how high we were. When the pilot made the airplane turn, I could feel my body being pushed toward the side of the plane. As we turned, we also tilted, with one wing of the plane going higher than the other wing. Instead of a steering wheel like a car did, the plane had a yoke that the pilot used to steer the plane. There was an extra yoke in front of my seat, and the pilot let me put my hands on it as it moved just like his yoke did in the turns. From that moment on, I WAS HOOKED ON FLYING!

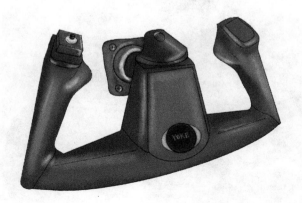

Parts of a plane

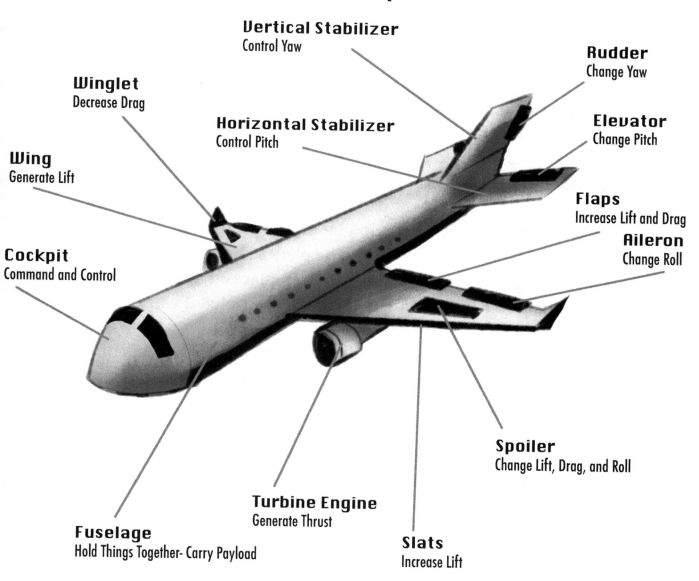

SONIC

Vertical Stabilizer
Control Yaw

Rudder
Change Yaw

Winglet
Decrease Drag

Horizontal Stabilizer
Control Pitch

Elevator
Change Pitch

Wing
Generate Lift

Flaps
Increase Lift and Drag

Aileron
Change Roll

Cockpit
Command and Control

Spoiler
Change Lift, Drag, and Roll

Turbine Engine
Generate Thrust

Slats
Increase Lift

Fuselage
Hold Things Together- Carry Payload

41

After I got back home, I started to learn about how airplanes were built. One of my favorite things to do was to build model airplanes. Daddy would bring me model airplane kits from his store. They would have sheets of thin, splintery wood called balsa wood, with patterns of the different parts of the plane stamped on them. I cut the shapes out then I would glue all the pieces together in the right places. Finally, I would cover the plane's skeleton with tissue paper, putting small dots of glue in certain places. I learned that if I sprayed the paper-covered model lightly with water, it would make the paper shrink tightly to the frame.

First time I did that, I went looking for something that could create a fine mist of water. "Oh, that's it," I thought, "Mother's perfume atomizer would be perfect!" I dumped the perfume out in the sink, filled the atomizer with water, and sprayed my model. Almost like magic, the paper shrank into place, and I held a tiny, beautiful airplane in my hand. I was so proud of my work that I ran to show it to Mother.

Mother thought the airplane was very nice, but she said, "If you had asked me about using my atomizer, we could have poured the perfume into another bottle and saved it." OOPS! I learned a lesson from that. I was just so EXCITED about my plane!

My parents loved me and treated me kindly. They taught me proper behavior, but they also let me explore things I was curious about. I grew up feeling that I could learn how to do anything I wanted to. And I learned the value of being careful and paying attention to instructions that someone told me or that I read, so I could understand how to do things the right way.

≥SONIC

Have you ever thought that building plastic model airplanes might be a fun hobby, but don't know where to start learning how to do it? There are four basic stages to building a plastic model airplane from a kit. They are planning, assembly, painting, and finishing. Here are some of the best model airplane kits on the market: Guillow's P-51 Mustang, Academy Models' WWII US Navy F6F, and Tamiya Models' Vought F4U-1D Corsair.

4

Records and Recognition

Dear Genius You,

Whatever you do, try as many things as you can, and do your best in everything you try! That's what I did, and you know what happened? I ended up being very good at lots of different things! The best rewards are always the ones you achieve because of your own merit and motivation. Now, here's my challenge to you: Go out there and do something that makes you feel ten feet tall today!

all the best,
Cutely

Besides airplanes, I was interested in many other things, mostly active things like playing music and competing in sports. I tried playing different instruments in the school band, and I finally settled on drums. More than a few times, I dreamed of being an orchestra conductor when I grew up.

I rode my horse, Victor, in rodeos. I especially liked barrel racing. Three barrels were set out in a large triangle shape. We had to run around each one in a certain order, going the right way around each barrel. Whoever did it fastest was the winner. I loved competing!

When I was twelve years old, I got a .22 rifle and joined the target shooting club at my school. I was the only girl on my five-person team that competed around New Mexico. I didn't mind being the only girl. I was used to it. The guys were used to me doing things with them. Our team was undefeated for my last two years in high school. The guys on other teams got a little embarrassed when a girl shot better than they did, but all I could ever think is, "Well, it is up to you to get better and practice more, instead of getting mad at me!"

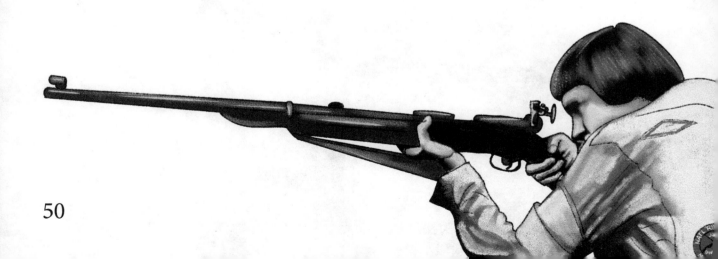

I practiced a lot and earned several rankings in target shooting. I completed the final one, Distinguished Rifleman, when I was barely sixteen. I had to shoot at targets 50 feet away, in four different positions—lying on my stomach, sitting, kneeling, and standing. All twenty of my shots were bullseyes. Mr. Bond, my instructor, sent the targets to the National Rifle Association in Washington, D.C., with my scores. The United States President, Dwight Eisenhower, wrote a letter congratulating me. What a thrill! Talk about PROUD! I was full to BURSTING!

I competed in skiing, too. When I was a junior in high school, I wanted to try out for the U.S. Junior Olympic Ski Team. I competed in downhill, slalom, and ski jumping.

When I started college, I decided to major in physical education because I loved being active and competing in sports. When Christmas break came during my first year at Stephen's College in Missouri, I went home to Taos and headed for the ski slopes. I was riding a ski lift up to the top of a trail when the cable suddenly popped loose and flipped me up into the air. The snow cushioned my fall a little, but I still landed hard. The snow was deep, and I sank down into it. People had a hard time finding me, even though I was yelling out at them. It seemed like I waited a long time for them to find me. When help finally arrived, I was very happy, and so I was smiling and joking while they carried me down the slope and put me in a car. I sat up while they drove me to my house, but I probably should have been lying down.

Mother took me to the emergency room. I had cracked a couple of bones in my back, and I had to wear a stiff brace until my back healed.

SONIC

Prior to the fall on the ski slope, it is very likely that Wally could have been a U.S. Olympian in skiing.

When I got back to school in Missouri, I couldn't do anything in my physical education classes because of my back brace. In truth, at that point I wasn't very interested in school. When the head of the college called Mother to inform her that he thought I could be doing better, she said, "Well don't you have an airport?"

He said, "Yes we do."

And Mother said, "Well, put her in those classes. She will be right at home there."

My mother was ahead of her time, and she loved me into the person I am today.

Cracking bones in my back during that fall on the ski slopes ended up being a kind of blessing in disguise. Once I switched from the physical education courses to the aviation courses, that's when I was standing knee deep in my joy! I finally learned to fly! I was no longer the little girl looking at the bolts on the tires or the nine year old in the co-pilot's seat, I WAS THE PILOT! Not only that, but I joined the flying team that competed in flying events against teams from other schools. And yes, I'm bragging…we usually won.

Stephens College was only a two-year school. After I finished there, I enrolled in Oklahoma State University. Their Flying Aggies was the best college aviation team in the country. I earned my way onto the team, and we kept on winning. I was on that team for two years, and both years we took first place in the big national competition. And both years I came away with trophies for the Flying Aggie Top Pilot and the Outstanding Female Pilot of the meet.

I had found what I wanted to do for the rest of my life: fly airplanes and teach other people how to fly, too. After I graduated from college, I got a job teaching people how to fly airplanes at an Army base in Oklahoma. I was flying every day and helping other people learn to soar in the clouds. OH, HOW I LOVED TO TEACH A PERSON TO FLY A PLANE!

SONIC

In 2010, Wally was inducted into the Oklahoma State University College of Education, Health, and Aviation Hall of Fame.

SUPERSONIC

After graduating from OSU in 1960, Funk made history as the military's first female civilian flight instructor.

HYPERSONIC

While at OSU, she flew at International Collegiate Air Meets and won awards such as Outstanding Female Pilot, Flying Aggie Top Pilot, and the Alfred Alder Memorial Trophy.

5

Mercury 13

Dear Genius You,

If ever you come across something and you see an opportunity, GRAB IT! Go for it with all of your might! You know what I think? I think we are supposed to be paying attention so when those opportunities are offered to us, we can take full advantage of them. There is an old saying that goes, "Luck is what happens when Preparation meets Opportunity." So be prepared when opportunity comes knocking ... and that's how you make your own luck.

All the best,

One day, I was looking at a magazine, and I saw a story about a woman named Jerrie Cobb. The story was called "Damp Prelude to Space." Under that headline, a smaller one said, "A potential lady orbiter excels in lonesome test." Pictures showed Jerrie floating in a tank of water. The story said she was being tested to see how long she could stand to be alone without seeing, hearing, tasting, smelling, or feeling anything.

I knew that seven men were training to be America's first people to fly into space. No one had ever done that before. And here in this magazine, a woman was being tested to become an astronaut. It wasn't just any woman, either: it was someone I knew. Jerrie Cobb was a famous pilot who also worked in Oklahoma. She and I both belonged to the Ninety-Nines, an organization for women fliers. Most pilots were men in those days.

Wow, I wanted in on this action! I figured if Jerrie could do it, I could do it too.

I wrote a letter to the doctor who was testing women pilots to see if they were healthy enough and strong enough to become astronauts. I told him about my flying experience and how I really wanted to fly in space. He wrote back and said I could come and take the tests. I was so excited! I started doing extra exercises every day to make myself stronger.

I got to Albuquerque, New Mexico, on a Sunday evening in February 1961. My motel was across the street from the Lovelace Clinic, where I would be taking my tests. The next morning, I walked across the street to get started.

SONIC

The Lovelace Clinic became known in the 1950s and 60s as the nation's premier center for aviation and space medicine research. Because commercial and Air Force pilots had been getting their physical exams there, it was chosen to test America's first candidates for space flight. In 1959, under contract with the newly formed NASA, Lovelace tested 32 candidate pilots using a seven-day series of rigorous physiological and psychological tests. After further testing in other places, the seven Project Mercury astronauts were chosen. A follow-up project demonstrated that women could pass the tests with approximately the same success rate as men. Dr. William Randolph "Randy" Lovelace II, the head of the clinic, was appointed by President Johnson as Director of Space Medicine for NASA in 1964.

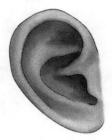

The doctors and nurses examined every part of my body more thoroughly than I had ever dreamed anyone would do. For five full days, I had more physical tests than I could count. They X-rayed every bone in my body and every tooth in my head. They checked my vision in daylight and in the dark. They measured how quickly I could see normally after the lights came back on. They tested my depth perception and my ability to focus my eyes on a moving object. They even took pictures of the insides of my eyeballs.

Some of the tests hurt. Truthfully, I was determined to endure whatever pain there was if it meant I could go to space. Once, they squirted very cold water into my ear for thirty seconds. That hurt a lot. It also numbed my inner ear so that I lost my sense of balance.

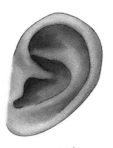

They measured how long it took for me to get back to normal. Then they gave me a chance to sit and rest for an hour. When they came back, they tested the other ear the same way. This time was worse because I already knew how much it was going to hurt. In another test, I had to ride an exercise bike until I got so tired I couldn't ride anymore. The bicycle was rigged so that it got harder and harder to pedal, like I was riding up a hill that got steeper and steeper. I made up my mind I would ride that bicycle longer than anyone had ever ridden it before. I pedaled and pedaled for eleven minutes. Finally, I had to stop. I was so tired that when I stepped off the bike, I fell flat on the floor!

After the week of testing was over, I went back to work in Oklahoma and waited to hear the results. Finally, I got a letter that said I had passed. Yes! I knew I could do it. I learned later that seventeen other women had taken all the same tests Jerrie and I took at the Lovelace Clinic. Thirteen of us had passed. The seven men who were training as America's first astronauts were known as the Mercury 7. We women became known as the Mercury 13. I liked the ring of that!

SUPERSONIC

America's first human space flight program was named Project Mercury, and so the seven astronauts chosen to fly in it were called the Mercury 7. On April 9, 1959, NASA announced their names: Scott Carpenter, Gordon Cooper, John Glenn, Gus Grissom, Wally Schirra, Alan Shepard, and Deke Slayton. All seven men got to fly in space in one of the 20th century NASA human spaceflight programs: Mercury, Gemini, Apollo, and the Space Shuttle.

Mercury 7
From Left to Right

Back Row: Alan Shepard, Gus Grissom, Gordon Cooper

Front Row: Wally Schirra, Deke Slayton, John Glenn, Scott Carpenter

HYPERSONIC

Jacqueline Cochran was one of the most accomplished pilots of the twentieth century. She was in her fifties when the Mercury 13 tests happened. Some of her famous firsts include being the first woman to pilot a bomber across the Atlantic Ocean, fly fast enough to break the sound barrier, land a plane relying only on her instruments, and land and take off again on an aircraft carrier. Together with Amelia Earhart, she opened the Bendix race to women, a race she flew in 1937 as the only female entrant. Also in 1937, Cochran set a new world's record for women's air speed. She led the WASPs (Women Airforce Service Pilots) in WWII. To this day, she is the only female president of the Fédération Aéronautique Internationale, the organization in charge of air sports.

The men who had become astronauts had gone other places to take different tests after they finished with the ones at the Lovelace Clinic. We women wanted to do that, too. We wanted to show that we could do just as well as the men could. And we really wanted to go into space!

After the first round of tests, I got a letter from Jackie Cochran, who had paid for our expenses in Albuquerque.

She said that twelve women had now been invited to the next round of tests, and that she was willing to help pay the travel and meal expenses for any of us who needed financial help. She wanted to support the program even though she was too old to be tested herself. She also wrote, "There is no astronaut program for women yet. The medical checks at Albuquerque and the further tests to be made at Pensacola are purely experimental and in the nature of research." She went on to say, "But I think a properly organized astronaut program for women would be a fine thing." Of course, I thought so, too. And I was a little surprised at her saying there was no astronaut program for women yet. Everyone at the Lovelace Clinic had talked like we were being evaluated as potential astronauts. It must be some formality of language, I thought.

Mercury 13
From Left to Right

Row 3: Gene Nora Stumbough, Sarah Gorelick, Jerrie Cobb, Irene Leverton, Jerri Truhill

Row 2: Janey Hart, Jean Hixson, Rhea Woltman, Bernice Steadman

Row 1: Myrtle Cagle, Wally Funk, Janet Dietrich, Marion Dietrich

6

Surpassing Scores

Dear Genius You,

Have you ever wanted something so much that you were willing to put in whatever work it would take to get you to that goal? Well, I knew I didn't just want to fly. I also wanted to go to space, and I did everything I could to make that dream possible. Just remember this: you must always work hard for what you are dreaming of, even if it takes a lifetime to achieve.

all the best,

In the meantime, I was already arranging for some other tests. The men's program consisted of physical fitness testing at the Lovelace Clinic (what we called Phase I), psychological and psychiatric evaluation at the Aero Medical Laboratory at Wright Field in Dayton, Ohio (Phase II), and physical stress tests at Wright Field (Phase III). Jerrie had completed the first phase in February 1960 in Albuquerque and tests similar to Phase II in September 1960 in Oklahoma City and Phase III in May 1961 in Pensacola. It was going to be a couple of months before my Phase III tests; so Jerrie helped me schedule the psychological phase starting on August 3, 1961, at the Veterans Administration Hospital in Oklahoma City with Dr. Jay T. Shurley. I was twenty-four years old now, and my flying hours were up to 4,600.

At this time, the only women I knew in the Mercury 13 were Jerrie and Gene Nora Stumbough. I had talked with Gene Nora about the tests in April 1961 at a Ninety-Nines meeting in Oklahoma City and suggested she apply. I knew she had won the Top Woman Pilot award at the 1959 NIFA meet where I had also done well. And as a student at the University of Oklahoma, she was currently the school's first female flight instructor.

I was tested for three days. The first two days were what you might expect for a psychological evaluation. The people who Interviewed me wanted to know about my life, my parents, my friends, my flying, anything I loved or hated. They couldn't quite understand that I didn't have any bad thoughts in my head. I was always happy. My parents were happy. I told them I wasn't afraid of anything!

I told them about my young life and the freedom I was given. They said, "What kind of music do you like?"

Rock and roll music was popular then, but I said, "I like opera." They said, "What's your favorite opera?"

"It's *Nabucco*," I said.

"Who wrote it?"

"Verdi."

Their mouths dropped open because I knew about operas. I GUESS they just didn't expect a girl like me to know about opera. Here's the thing…NEVER UNDERESTIMATE ANYBODY! I liked opera and airplanes and going fast! Listen to an overture of Giuseppe Verdi sometime…those operatic numbers can go nearly as fast as I can fly!

SONIC

Opera is a dramatic story told entirely through song. It is based on the feeling that music can communicate people's reactions and emotions better than words or pictures.

SUPERSONIC

Giuseppe Verdi was a young musical prodigy. His musical training began at the local church, where he was the full-time organist at only nine years old. In 1823, at just 10 years old, he became heavily involved in the city's musical life both as a composer and as a performer.

HYPERSONIC

The opera *Nabucco* tells the story of a struggle for power, religion, and love between two opposing forces, the Israelites and Babylonians, in the fifth century B.C.E. Please listen, it really gets me going!

All the time the doctors were interviewing me, they were putting a thermometer in my mouth every two hours, and they would dutifully write down the results. I asked why, and they said I would find out eventually.

They gave me so many tests! On the Rorschach test, I had to describe what I saw in some ink blots. In another test, they showed me a picture and told me to make up a story about it. I had to draw a person, complete a sentence, and fill out a long form selecting my preferences about lots of things. There were tests about mathematical reasoning and understanding mechanical things. I can't remember them all. The tests tired my brain, and when I got back to Jerrie Cobb's house, where I stayed during the testing, in the evening we would do physical exercises so I could stay in shape and unwind.

⫸SONIC

A Rorschach test uses inkblots to help patients form associations in their minds. It was developed by Swiss doctor Hermann Rorschach in the 1920s.

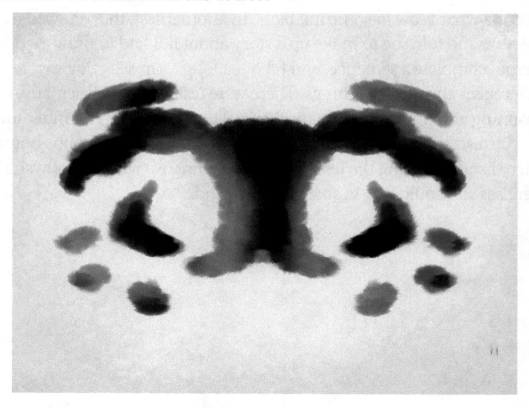

At the end of the second day, the doctors said, "Tomorrow, bring your swimsuit. We have a chamber of water that we want you to go in." The next morning, I went to the hospital and changed into my swimsuit. The doctors pointed to a door and told me there was a tank of water in the next room. They gave me two pieces of foam rubber, each about the size of a brick. I was to put one of them behind my neck and one under the small of my back and then float on the water, face up.

They said, "You're going to have ear plugs to keep the water out of your ears, and the lights are going to be turned off. We want you to be very careful getting into this pool. We want you to lie there. Don't try to do anything; don't try to swim. Just lie there for as long as you can." Before I went through the door, I saw there was a clock above it. It was 8:30 in the morning. I went in and found this great big steel tank, about eight feet across and eight feet deep. I climbed up the steps and got into the pool.

I was going to have to stay still in the water, or the foam pieces would shift out from under me. The pictures I saw in *Life* magazine of Jerrie in the tank showed that she had an inflated rubber collar around her neck and large pieces of foam rubber strapped around her hips. But I wasn't worried about these small pieces I had. I grew up swimming and soaking in the hot springs in Taos. I was used to being in the water.

They turned the lights off, and it became absolutely dark. It was like my eyes were lined with black velvet. I couldn't see anything, and the doctors couldn't see me. It was also completely quiet in the room—not a sound. Well, that's not quite true—I could hear a tiny whisper with each breath I exhaled. I wondered if I would be able to hear my own heartbeats, but I never did. I couldn't feel any air movement. I couldn't smell anything. I spread my arms out to the sides; that seemed to make me feel most comfortable. After a couple of minutes I thought, something is wrong here. I can't feel a thing. I slapped the surface of the water, BUT I COULDN'T FEEL IT! I patted my face with my wet hand, and I couldn't feel the water on my face! I brought my hand up and dripped water from my fingers onto my face. I couldn't feel the drops.

Ah, now I realized why they had taken my temperature so often. They figured out my average body temperature and made the water and the air in that room exactly that temperature. It was humid enough that the water on my face didn't evaporate and cool my skin. I felt like I was floating in nothing. I was in space! A microphone was hanging a couple of inches above me so the doctors could monitor my breathing. Some people who had taken this test in the past couldn't stand the lack of physical sensations and started to hallucinate. The microphone would alert the doctors if I got into trouble and needed to get out quickly. They told me I could talk to them as much as I wanted, to share my thoughts or just have the comfort of talking to someone. I don't think I talked at all during the test. I didn't have anything to say.

I just lay there and lay there. I thought about things I had done in the past and what my future might be. I thought about being here, taking these tests, and possibly becoming an astronaut. I thought about what great parents I had bringing me up. I had a horse back in Taos, and I was doing well in my flying. I was not bored lying there. I thought about everything, and I thought about nothing. I just felt comfortable…at peace…imagining that floating like this might be what it would feel like to float in space. Life was incredibly exciting and satisfying, and I think I even dozed off a couple of times.

After a while, I heard a voice. One of the doctors said, "Wally, how do you feel?"

"I feel fantastic."

"Are you hungry?"

"Nope."

"Do you have to go to the bathroom?"

I said, "I already did that." My goodness, I'd been lying in a tank of warm water for several hours. What did he expect?

Then he said, "We're going to turn the lights on very slowly. Get a towel on you and come on out. Be very careful getting over the top of the tank."

So, I moved over to the place where I could reach the steps and get out of the pool. I put the towel around me and came out of the room. I turned around to look at the clock, and they had covered it up! I had no idea how long I had been in the tank. I guessed it was about four or five hours.

I went into the adjoining dressing room and put my clothes on. I came back out and sat down with the doctors. They said, "Wally, you stayed in ten hours and thirty-five minutes."

I said, "Holy cow." It didn't feel like that. It turned out that was a new record! Jerrie had stayed in nine hours and forty minutes before they told her that was long enough and that she should come out. Another Mercury 13 gal, Rhea Hurrle, had stayed in for ten hours until they told her to stop.

I spent another half hour answering questions. Where was I, and why was I there? What did I feel while I was in the tank? Some of the questions were the same ones they had asked during the last two days. I guess they wanted to see if I had changed my mind about my parents, my school, whatever. No, I hadn't changed my mind about anything.

Jerrie, Rhea, and I had all passed a much more difficult isolation test than the male astronaut candidates had. They just sat at a desk alone in a dark, soundproof room for two or three hours. They could walk around or sit at a chair at a desk in the room. John Glenn even said later that he found some paper in the desk drawer and wrote poetry in the dark to occupy himself. Being able to do nothing but float in water that we could not feel was certainly more like being in a space capsule without normal gravity.

After passing that test with flying colors, I knew down deep in my bones that Jerrie, Rhea, myself, and the rest of the Mercury 13 were just as space worthy as the men astronauts.

7

Throw it a Fish

Dear Genius You,

What I have to tell you next may seem discouraging, but don't you dare let it! THROW IT A FISH! In fact, this fish might have been the biggest one I've ever thrown in my life. You'll see what I mean as you read this next bit about what happened for me and my Mercury 13 friends. But, listen up! NEVER, EVER, EVER GIVE UP! Even Einstein himself said, "If at first, the idea is not absurd enough, then there is no hope for it!" Meaning no matter how crazy it sounds to everybody else, you just keep hoping for what everyone else thinks is impossible! WHEEEEE!

all the best,

returned to work at Fort Sill, but I was looking forward to the Phase III tests that were scheduled to start September 18. A week before I planned to leave for Pensacola, I received a telegram from Dr. Lovelace. It said,

SERVICE		TELEGRAM	DATE
✕✕✕		⊗	X-✕X-✕X

±obdobq=ql ⇌as f pb⇌oo^kdbj bkqp⇌q=nbkp^`1 i ^=
`^k` bi ba=mol _^_i v=t fi i =kl q=_b=ml ppf_i b=ql =
`^oov∓r q=qe f p=m̂oq=nc=xëáÅz=mol do^j =vl r =
j ^v=obqr ok=bunbkpb=^as^k` b=^i i l qj bkq=ql =
i l s bi ^` b=cl r ka^qf l k=` Ll =j b=i bqqbo∓fi i =
^as f pb∓c⇌aaf qf l k^i ⇌abs bi l mj bkqp=t ebk=
j ^qqbo=`i b^oba=cr oqeboK≤

93

Jerrie's assistant also sent a telegram that said,

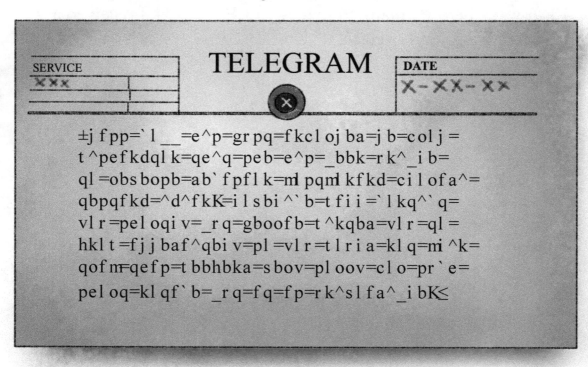

TELEGRAM

SERVICE
XXX

DATE
X-XX-XX

±j f pp=`l __ =e^p=gr pq=f kcl oj ba=j b=col j =
t ^pef kdql k=qe^q=peb=e^p=_bbk=r k^_i b=
ql =obs bopb=ab`f pfl k=ml pqml kfkd=ci l of a^=
qbpqfkd=^d^f kK=i l s bi ^` b=t fi i =`l kq^` q=
vl r =pel oqi v=_ r q=gboofb=t ^kqba=vl r =ql =
hkl t =fj j baf ^qbi v=pl =vl r =t l r i a=kl q=mi ^k=
qof m=qefp=t bbhbka=s bov=pl oov=cl o=pr ` e=
pel oq=kl qf` b=_ r q=fq=fp=r k^sl f a^_i bK≤

I was stunned. I was looking forward to that experience so much, and I had worked so hard to be ready for it. I didn't know the reason for the cancellation at that time, but I learned more about it later. Dr. Lovelace had been doing the women's tests without NASA's involvement. The expenses were paid by the Lovelace Foundation and Jackie Cochran and her husband, not the government.

Apparently, someone had questioned whether NASA had approved the women's tests at the Naval Air Station in Pensacola and whether the costs were justified. NASA declined to authorize them, and the Navy withdrew permission to use its facilities.

I was very disappointed, no doubt about that. But I wasn't going to sit back and sulk over it. I was young and happy, and I believed I would eventually go into space. So, I just THREW IT A FISH and went on with my life. I figured I would find an alternate path. Nearly a year later, in July 1962, Jerrie Cobb and another Mercury 13 member challenged NASA in a Congressional hearing. The other woman, Janey Hart, was the oldest of the Mercury 13 and the wife of U.S. Senator Philip Hart of Michigan. With the help of her husband's connections, a special subcommittee of the U.S. House of Representatives' Committee on Science and Astronautics agreed to hold a public hearing to examine whether NASA had discriminated against women in the selection of Mercury astronauts.

Jerrie and Janey made strong arguments, testifying about the great performance of the Mercury 13 in the Lovelace exams, Jerrie's success with the Pensacola tests, and the records she, Rhea, and I had set in the isolation tests. NASA had John Glenn testify and say that men went to war, men flew planes, and men went to space. And that in a nutshell was the end of the possibility of the Mercury 13 to become astronauts at that time.

SONIC

Only Cobb had actually been allowed to finish all three phases of the physical testing. She had passed with scores that rivaled those of one of the Mercury 7's top scorers, John Glenn, but it didn't matter.

SUPERSONIC

In May of 1961, President John Kennedy stood up before a joint session of Congress and announced that the United States was going to the moon. For NASA, after that, there was no longer room for experimenting; everything was focused on the goal of landing the first humans on the moon.

HYPERSONIC

John Glenn was a national hero and an astronaut, and his words carried enormous weight. In that meeting before the subcommittee, John Glenn argued that testing women or doing anything that took funding away from the main mission to go to the moon was a waste of time and resources. "I think this gets back to the way our social order is organized," Glenn told the subcommittee. "It is just a fact. The men go off and fight the wars and fly the airplanes and come back and help design and build and test them. The fact that women are not in this field is a fact of our social order." The subcommittee sided with Glenn.

Boy, were his words a real kick in the pants! Just like Jerrie, I did as well or better than the Mercury 7 astronauts! I passed all the tests I took, and I eventually applied to become an astronaut for NASA. I applied four times, but they always said "no." Finally, they said I couldn't be an astronaut because I didn't have a college degree in engineering. That is why I now tell young people, especially girls, to study STEM subjects.

Every time NASA said "NO," I was deeply disappointed. But I knew what I had to do. I THREW IT A FISH! If NASA wouldn't let me be an astronaut for them, I would find some other way to get into space.

And again, I want to tell you…YES, I WAS DISAPPOINTED, but I was never bitter. I was brought up that when things don't work out, you let it pass and keep moving forward. I didn't have the Lovelace Program anymore, but I had the Wally Funk Program. I realized I still had a lot to do and achieve, and I would find a way to get into space.

8

Searching for Space

Dear Genius You,

Hey, you are really hanging in here with me! What is it that you are searching for? Art, Music, Sports, Science, Engineering, Design, Computing? It makes me no never mind what it is you are searching for. I just want to encourage you to search for it with all your heart.

All the best,
Purely

That fall, I relocated to California. I got a job with Wright's Flying Service at the airport in Hawthorne. I had flown in and out of that airport several times, and on one visit, I asked if they needed a flight instructor. They did, and I got the job. I also flew charter flights for them and served as chief pilot of Wright's Flying Service. That meant I had to make sure the aircraft were properly maintained and the other pilots were well trained. I was responsible for keeping up to date with state and federal regulations and making sure we were in compliance. As an instructor and charter pilot, I was flying seven or eight hours a day and loving it.

I bought myself a Stearman, a 1940s-era biplane with an open cockpit. It had a 250-horsepower engine in it, and it was great for doing acrobatics. I learned to do all kinds of loops and rolls, and I taught some students how to do acrobatics, too. In the years since then, I have owned three other airplanes, all Cessnas—a 182, a 172, and a 150.

One day, a DC-3 was sitting at the Hawthorne airport. I asked for the key for it. It was a commercial airplane that could hold about twenty passengers, but I was by myself. I knew I could fly it. I went up and down the runway, just taxiing. Finally, the tower said, "When do you think you're going to take off?" I said, "Now."

I got in position and took off. It was heavier than my little Stearman; so it took a little longer on the runway. It had more power because it had two engines, and I had to use more of the right rudder because the propellers both rotated in the same direction. I took off, and I was climbing up. "Holy cow! I got up, now I've got to get down without hurting it!" I thought. I went out over the ocean again and did more maneuvers. You can't do loops in that aircraft. I just did a lot of different turns and altitude changes to get the feel of the plane.

I came back to the tower, and I said, "I want to make a couple of low passes and see how I feel with the power situation. Then I'll try to set it down, and if it's good, then I'll put the tail wheel down." The best way to do it is to have all three wheels down at the same time, but I didn't have enough experience in that heavy of an airplane. I lined up with the runway and held the wings level. As I got closer, I was feeling good about being in control of the plane. I eased off on the power and touched the front wheels down. As I slowed more, the tail wheel touched down, too.

I did it. I pulled it off! I knew I could do it, but that doesn't mean I took it for granted that I would land easily. I used all my flying experience to be sure I was controlling that plane safely. The safe landing was a relief, but not a surprise.

SONIC

Air traffic control gives aircraft permission for takeoff or landing, ensuring that there is always enough room on the runway between aircraft. Pilots often call air traffic control "tower" or "tower control."

SUPERSONIC

To land any aircraft, you have to slow down and descend to the runway. You can lower speed by reducing thrust and increasing drag using flaps, landing gear, or speed brakes.

HYPERSONIC

Pilots say that takeoff is optional, but landing is mandatory. Good landings result from good approaches. It's true. On the final approach, you want to be flying at a constant target airspeed, constant target descent rate, and constant target power setting. This way, you're on a stabilized flight path to the touchdown point, a point, by the way, that should be within the first third of the runway's length. All that remains for you to do is concentrate on any wind corrections, check for any deviations from the stabilized profile, and reduce power.

I was young and confident, and I felt like I could do anything I wanted to do. That was my attitude about becoming an astronaut, too. The Lovelace women astronaut program was over, but that didn't stop me. I made up my mind to make my own arrangements to take as many Phase III-type tests as I could. I knew people in the military from my time at Fort Sill and my time working in Southern California. In August of 1962, because of my qualifications and reputation, I got permission to go to El Toro Marine Corps Air Station near Irvine, California, and take two tests. I was the first woman to get this permission.

The first test was the Martin-Baker ejection seat test. I was wearing a flight suit, and a couple of Marines strapped me into an airplane ejection seat that was mounted on a long, almost vertical track. I pulled a support up over my helmet to keep my head held firmly against the head rest so that my head wouldn't come forward, because you could break your neck. They shot me up that pole, probably around twenty feet, and I came down with a terrible thud.

I didn't realize the consequences, but the guys knew. I would have a tremendous headache, and I could have a back compression. Well, I had never told anybody I had hurt my back skiing, trying to prepare for the Olympics. I thought, "Uh-oh. I wonder if anything has happened here," but nothing happened. My back was fine.

I said, "Wow, you guys, I have a big, big headache."

They said, "We're going to help you get rid of that. We're going to take you to the high-altitude chamber test."

I walked into this chamber at El Toro. Two doctors came in with me. I sat at one end of the chamber by a console, and one of the doctors said, "You're supposed to punch out lights that come on, write your name and anything else you want, and add some numbers on this piece of paper."

I put on an oxygen mask, and they started to reduce the pressure in the air to match what it would be at increasing altitudes. We zoomed on up there. I think it was to the equivalent of about 30,000 feet. And, boy, on 100 percent oxygen, I was feeling great. They say that breathing 100 percent oxygen is just the best way to get rid of a headache. Then came the real test.

A voice said, "Wally, take your mask off."

So, I took my oxygen mask off.

"We want you to keep writing and pushing the lights."

I was just blithely writing things down and doing my assignment, thinking I was doing a great job. Things got a little gray. I was still writing and pushing out buttons, but I didn't realize I was getting slower

Pretty soon, I heard something, but I didn't react to it.

Someone said, "Wally, put your mask on. Wally, put your mask on!"

Then a doctor came over and put it on me. "Oh my," I thought. "Oh, my word! Color!" Color was coming back. All the faces were coming back. I was amazed how my brain did not work without enough oxygen. But now I was back to normal.

One of the doctors said, "Do you need help getting out?"

I said, "No, I think I'm all right." I walked out and went around where they wanted to show me something.

They said, "Do you want to see a film of how you looked in there?"

I said, "Yeah!" In the film, I could see myself with my mask off, writing on a clipboard. It was all scribbles, and I was writing way off the page into the air.

Another time I went into a high-altitude chamber. It was a room where I put on an oxygen mask and they pumped some of the oxygen out of the room. It was like being in an airplane 30,000 feet in the air. There isn't enough oxygen in the air at that altitude.

I thought I was doing just really terrific, because you feel a sense of well-being when your brain is low on oxygen. This is why a lot of airplane pilots have accidents. They have a feeling of euphoria, but because they're not getting enough oxygen to the brain to read their instrumentation correctly, they get into trouble. That high-altitude chamber test was a valuable experience for me. Being without enough oxygen had really made my brain do silly things! That taught me a very important lesson about wearing an oxygen mask when I flew my airplane high into the sky. And it made me realize how important a space suit would be if I flew even higher into space.

The following year, I was able to arrange to take a centrifuge test at the University of Southern California. Being a civilian and being a woman, I could not have a G suit to help keep the blood pushed up to my brain. Only men could have those things. But tight suits? Come on! Women had been squeezing into tight underclothes for a long time! So, I called Mother up in Hemet, California and said, "Mom, can I borrow your corset and girdle? Can you get those to me?"

She said, "You betcha."

I made my own G suit out of her corset and girdle, stuffed my body in this tight little thing, and put my flight suit over it. I knew that the examiners thought once they started to twirl me around in the centrifuge, I was going to pass out within the first experience of 5 Gs. But I knew to keep the blood pushed up in my head.
They strapped me in the centrifuge seat. We started the first run. I was sitting down, and it started to go round and round. Man, I was happy as a clam! I kept my head straight and steady. I had to push out some buttons because they wanted to see how I would do. Doing acrobatics in the Stearman, I had been doing 360s (turning a full circle horizontally, almost like a centrifuge), which is about 4 Gs. I know because I had a G-meter in the cockpit. So, this was no big deal to me.

SONIC

Fighter pilots wear G suits to combat gravity. When they are under positive G forces, the suit inflates to keep blood from staying in their feet and legs, which could cause them to pass out.

SUPERSONIC

G force means the values of force and acceleration. Astronauts, fighter pilots, and Formula One drivers might experience a force of so many "Gs" when going fast or turning quickly. When an astronaut alters trajectory, a pilot changes speed or direction, or a racing driver goes around a corner, the strength of the forces involved can be several times higher than the Earth's gravitational force. Then they experience 2 Gs (2 times the force of gravity), 3 Gs, 4 Gs, and so on. High G forces can make it hard for humans to breathe and can cause unconsciousness by keeping blood from reaching the brain.

HYPERSONIC

Wally made her own G suit out of her mom's corset and girdle. Wally Wisdom: There is always a way! Sometimes you just have to engineer the solution yourself!

We went a second run of 5 Gs. No big deal. I punched out the buttons of lights that were coming up for my assignments. We went a third run, no problem. I was feeling a little tired, but it was okay. When we did the fourth run, I don't know if the guy really hit the button and gave me a few more Gs or if it was the same number of Gs but my body not having a rest in between runs. I could tell I needed to keep the blood up to my brain; so, I just tensed up my body and my neck and pushed all that blood back up in my head. Then I just kept doing my thing, and I passed with flying colors. I never told the examiners that I had made my own G suit. It didn't come out until a *Dateline* television interview I did more than twenty years later.

I took my centrifuge test at USC in mid-March 1963. Three months later, the Soviets sent the first woman into space. Cosmonaut Valentina Tereshkova flew into orbit for three days, circling the Earth forty-eight times. It turned out to be just a publicity stunt because the USSR didn't fly another woman into space until nineteen years later. But publicity was important during the Cold War, and just think: my fellow Mercury 13 gals and I could have been the first women in space. The truth is I knew I had what it took to be an astronaut. I knew it down deep in the marrow of my being. Sooner or later, I would get to space, with or without NASA. In the meantime, there was a great big ole life out there for me to live…so I got busy doing just that.

9

Taking Charge

Dear Genius You,

Has anyone ever told you that YOU are in charge of your own dreams? Well, while that may sound a bit scary, it is most certainly the truth. But instead of being afraid of that truth, how about you wrap your arms around that thought and let it excite you about what you can do when you put your mind to it? Sound like a plan? YES, IT DOES! Yes, it does indeed!

all the best,

had made up my mind to take charge of getting myself into space, but I also knew I had a full life to live. There were other things I wanted to do, too, and ways I wanted to help other people. I took charge of those parts of my life, too.

All my life, I have earned my living as a pilot and flight instructor. I love flying, and I love teaching other people to fly airplanes. I have worked at airports all over the United States and have even taught a few people to fly in other countries. I love traveling and seeing different places, too!

Once, I was going to apply for a new job that sounded interesting. I asked a man I knew to write a letter of recommendation for me. He worked for the Federal Aviation Administration (FAA). He asked me to come to his office and meet with him. After we talked for a while, he asked me if I would like to work as an aviation inspector for the FAA. I would be the first woman hired to do that job. Well, I grabbed that opportunity!

I started that job in 1971. One of my duties was to go to flight schools and inspect their operations. Were they taking good care of their airplanes to make sure they worked right and were safe to fly? Were they teaching their students all they needed to know to be careful pilots and fly safely?

Another part of my job was to give check rides to people who were trying to get their pilot's license. I would sit beside them in the airplane while they flew, and I watched to make sure they knew how to do everything a pilot needs to do.

I had been working for the FAA for four years when I got a phone call from another man I knew. He worked for the National Transportation Safety Board (NTSB). He asked me if I would like to work as an Air Safety Investigator for the NTSB. Again, I would be the first woman hired to do that job. Guess what…. I grabbed that opportunity, too!

For the next ten years, I would go to places where an airplane had just crashed. It was my job to figure out why the crash happened. It was like being a detective. I had to look for clues in the pieces of the airplane and in marks on the trees or the ground. Sometimes, I found that a part of the plane had stopped working right. Other times, the plane was overloaded and too heavy to fly right. Or the pilot made a bad mistake.

I wasn't trying to point the finger and blame anyone for a crash. The FAA took the information we investigators learned about how crashes happened and used it to teach other pilots how to not let the same thing happen to them. I like helping people and keeping people safe.

SONIC

The Federal Aviation Administration is part of the United States Department of Transportation. It keeps track of airspace and aircraft within the United States, and it also creates safe standards for aircraft.

SUPERSONIC

The National Transportation Safety Board (NTSB) finds out why crashes happen and helps prevent them.

HYPERSONIC

Regular inspections help aircraft work properly. Without them, planes could wear out and crash. Inspections before and after flying make sure the plane is safe and let the pilot and the mechanics know if anything needs to be fixed.

My aviation work was fun and interesting, but I also kept looking for ways to get into space. I had a special opportunity in 1988. I belong to the Ninety-Nines. It's an organization for women pilots, and it has members all over the world.

SONIC

The Ninety-Nines is an organization of women pilots founded in 1929 in New York. The name comes from the 99 original members. Amelia Earhart became the group's first president in 1931.

SUPERSONIC

Other women soon joined the Ninety-Nines as they became licensed pilots. In recent years, women student pilots have become members.

HYPERSONIC

The Ninety-Nines have a group song!

SONG OF THE NINETY-NINES
Written in 1941 by Dick Ballou

"In the air, everywhere,
It's the song of The Ninety-Nines.
Wings in Flight,
Day and Night,
with the Song of The Ninety-Nines;
On the line,
fliers fine,
ships and spirits tuned in rhyme,
Keep that formation
over the nation
with the song of The Ninety-Nines."

126

A group of us Ninety-Nines from the United States were invited to visit members in Russia. During our meetings, I gave a talk about American women in space. I spoke about my own experiences as one of the Mercury 13, and I talked about other women who had actually become astronauts and flown in our space shuttle program. During that trip, one of my big dreams came true. I met Russian cosmonaut Valentina Tereshkova (the Russians call their astronauts "cosmonauts"). She had been the first woman in space. In 1963, two years after I took the astronaut physical tests, she flew a spaceship for her country. She spent almost three full days in space, flying around the Earth forty-eight times. I had wanted to meet her ever since then. We sat and talked for more than half an hour. What a thrill!

A few years later, I grabbed another opportunity. I spent three days at the Space Academy in Huntsville, Alabama. It was like going to camp to train as an astronaut. I learned some amazing things about gravity. The gravity on the Moon is only one-sixth as strong as gravity on Earth. I would have to struggle to lift a sixty-pound object on Earth. But on the Moon, I would be able to lift it easily because it would feel like it weighed only ten pounds. The camp had a special piece of equipment that let me feel like I was working without any gravity. Astronauts working outside their ship in space would feel that way. I sat in a chair that floated across the floor on a cushion of air. The chair could also move up, down, and around when I pushed very lightly on another object.

When I tried to turn a nut with a wrench, the nut wouldn't turn, but I would start spinning! Haha! Proof that ole Mr. Newton knew what he was talking about when he said: "For every action there is an equal and opposite reaction." What a hoot to experience that law firsthand! Astronauts have to learn different ways to work in space.

In 2000, I had a chance to go to Russia and spend five days experiencing some of the rigorous training their cosmonauts get. I got to wear one of the space suits they use. I learned how their spaceships work. The most fun was getting to float like astronauts do in space. I climbed into a big airplane that had no seats for passengers. There was just an open space like a large room. The pilot flew the plane steeply up into the sky, then turned and flew down steeply (called Parabolic Flight Maneuvers). While we were going down, I floated just like there was no gravity! The pilot flew those up-and-down arcs ten times, and each time I floated for half a minute. I could push myself off one end of the room and fly across it like Superman. I could turn somersaults in midair. It was such a free feeling!

SUPERSONIC

Microgravity flight is the only way to achieve weightlessness, and it only lasts 20-30 seconds at a time. The Zero G company offers flights and opportunities for students.

10

Astronauts

Dear Genius You,

Have you ever thought about being an astronaut? Would you like to be one? Would you rather design the rockets that help humans go back to the moon and on to Mars? Or do you want to be in Mission Control supporting the astronauts who are in space? Maybe you want to gaze up at the stars and figure out what is out there. Just remember, astronauts are just regular people who love science, who love exploration, and who never gave up on their dreams.

All the best,

Astronauts are special people. They are smart and well educated, and they have a lot of practical experience, especially with flying airplanes. They are also brave. Being blasted into space on top of a rocket is dangerous, but space explorers are willing to take the chance because they know that space exploration is important. Plus, they trust the people who design, build, and operate the rockets and spaceships.

SONIC SUPERSONIC HYPERSONIC

Benefits of Space Exploration:

Health Care: Experiments performed in space help us understand health problems on Earth.

The Environment: Satellites provide data on climate change, measure pollution, and help protect our planet.

Inventions: Space technologies improve products we use every day, weather forecasts, and communications worldwide.

Safety: Satellite data can be used to predict natural disasters and to support emergency relief efforts.

Scientific Discoveries: Scientific breakthroughs are challenging our assumptions and pushing our boundaries by exploring the unknown.

Inspiration: Space Science and Space Exploration encourage young people to study STEM subjects and innovate the future.

Within the next few decades, humans could be leaving their footprints on Mars! But sooner than that, NASA's Artemis program will land the first woman and the next man on the Moon. The Orion spacecraft atop the Space Launch System (SLS) rocket will carry humans farther into space than they have gone before—for missions to the Moon and eventually to Mars. We will need even more astronauts!

So, what does it take to be an astronaut? I certainly always felt that I had the RIGHT STUFF. The astronaut requirements have changed with NASA's goals and missions. Today, to be considered for an astronaut position, applicants must meet the following qualifications:

• Be a U.S. citizen.

• Possess a master's degree in a STEM field, including engineering, biological science, physical science, or computer science or mathematics from an accredited institution. The master's degree requirement can also be met by:

> • Two years (36 semester hours or 54 quarter hours) of work toward a doctoral program in a related science, technology, engineering or math field.
>
> • A completed Doctor of Medicine or Doctor of Osteopathic Medicine degree.

• Complete a nationally recognized test pilot school program. Have at least two years of related professional experience obtained after degree completion or at least 1,000 hours pilot-in-command time on jet aircraft.

•Be able to pass the NASA long-duration flight astronaut physical. Astronaut candidates must also have skills in leadership, teamwork and communications.

NASA's Astronaut Selection Board reviews the applications and ranks each candidate's qualifications. The board then invites a small group of the most highly qualified candidates for interviews at NASA's Johnson Space Center in Houston, Texas. Of those interviewed, about half are invited back for second interviews. From that group, NASA's new astronaut candidates are selected. They report for training at Johnson and spend the next two years learning basic astronaut skills like spacewalking, operating the space station, flying T-38 jet planes, and controlling a robotic arm.

Boy oh boy, doesn't that sound like the MOST FUN EVER? With NASA's plans for the future of exploration, new astronauts will fly farther into space than ever before on lunar missions and may be the first humans to fly on to Mars…maybe we will go together!

I have been able to meet many astronauts because of my experience as a Mercury 13 member and because of my continuing efforts to fly into space. The first one I met was Scott Carpenter. He was one of America's first astronauts, the Mercury 7, and he was the second American to fly a spaceship in Earth orbit. His trip took him around the world three times in 1962. That was just a year after I took the tests at the Lovelace Clinic. We didn't meet until 1973, when I was going to New York to be interviewed on a television show.

Another astronaut I've met a few times is Buzz Aldrin. He was one of the first two men who walked on the Moon in July 1969. When Buzz and Scott were astronauts, NASA wasn't hiring any women to fly in space. That didn't happen until 1978, when NASA picked six women and twenty-nine men for America's sixth group of astronauts. One of those women was Sally Ride. She became the first American woman to fly in space in 1983 when she did science experiments on a space shuttle flight. I met Sally, too.

SONIC

Astronaut, engineer, and fighter pilot Buzz Aldrin made three spacewalks during the Gemini 12 mission in 1966. In 1969, he and Neil Armstrong were the first two humans to set foot on the Moon during the Apollo 11 mission.

SUPERSONIC
Sally Ride and Mae Jemison

Sally Ride was among the first women astronauts NASA chose in 1978, and in 1983 at the age of 32, she became the first American woman to fly in space. She remains the youngest NASA astronaut to have gone to space.

Mae Jemison was the first African American female astronaut and the first African American woman in space. She flew on the space shuttle Endeavor for eight days in 1992. In addition to being an astronaut, Jemison is also an engineer, physician, educator, and dancer.

One of the astronauts I've gotten to know best is Eileen Collins. She was the first female pilot NASA hired as an astronaut. She went into space four times, flying space shuttles in orbit around the Earth. She invited the members of the Mercury 13 to watch her launch into space in 1995 as the first woman pilot of a space shuttle. A rocket launched her spaceship at night, and it was a beautiful, bright sight. I was so excited and proud to see a female finally piloting a spaceship for NASA. As the rocket roared up into the sky, I pumped my arms into the air and yelled, "Go, Eileen! Go for all of us!"

HYPERSONIC

Eileen Collins is a Groundbreaking, Record Setting, Trail Blazing, SPACE BLAZING Female Role Model! Even when she was very young and first started reading about astronauts, one thing was very evident to Eileen: there were no WOMEN astronauts. She was incredibly inspired by the MALE Mercury astronauts, and by the time she was in high school and college, new opportunities were opening up for women in aviation. Her timing and her path seemed to align with the stars, because upon joining the Air Force, during her first month of training, her base was visited by the newest astronaut class—the first to include women. Her trajectory and purpose were evident. Though dozens of women have flown on the space shuttle during the course of its 30-year career, only two have commanded the spaceship, NASA astronauts Eileen Collins and Pamela Melroy.

Perhaps the thing that is most impressive and endearing about Eileen Collins is her generosity of heart and the awareness she had for the women who had gone before her and made her dream possible. A beneficiary of the efforts of the Mercury 13, Eileen was the first female to pilot a space shuttle in 1995 as well as the first to serve as shuttle commander in 1999. Eileen has said that being in the space program, working for NASA, and being an astronaut is the greatest adventure on this planet—or off the planet. She really wanted to fly the space shuttle…and so she did. To read more about Astronaut Eileen Collins, check out her book *Through the Glass Ceiling To the Stars: The Story of the First American Woman to Command A Space Mission.*

11

Always Looking Up

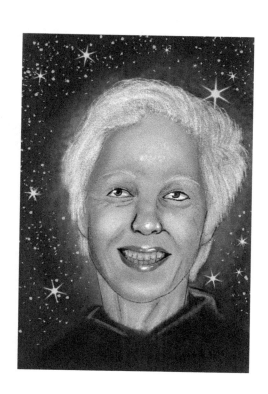

Dear Genius You,

Always, Always, Keep Looking Up! Look for the positives, eliminate the negatives, and keep heading in the direction of every dream you can dream!

All the best,

Dudley

In the 1990s, some companies started trying to build rockets and spaceships using their own ideas. Before that, they had only built rockets and spaceships the way NASA wanted them. Companies building different kinds of rockets meant there might be other ways to fly into space besides being a NASA astronaut.

One of the companies that was trying to build its own spaceship was called Vela Technology Development. Some people came and told me about how it would get into space for a suborbital flight. Riding inside the ship, I would be above the Earth's atmosphere, and the sky wouldn't be blue anymore. It would be black. I would be able to look out the window and see part of the Earth below me, looking like a huge ball. I said yes, I wanted to go when they had the spaceship ready to fly. A few years went by, and they never finished building it. I was disappointed, but I just threw it a fish.

SONIC

A suborbital flight is a quick trip up into space and right back down to Earth. An orbital spaceflight launches a vehicle at a high enough speed to send it into space for at least one full trip around the Earth. Simply put, suborbital goes up and down, while orbital goes around. Virgin Galactic can now take six passengers at a time on its SpaceShipTwo vehicle, giving customers a few minutes of microgravity at 50 miles up in space. Blue Origin has also flown commercial spaceflight passengers on its New Shepard rocket at 65 miles above the Earth.

SUPERSONIC

Space Perspectives plans to offer balloon rides to the edge of space! Its Neptune capsule shows people the curve of the earth and the blackness of space.

HYPERSONIC

Overview Effect

More than 30 years ago, Frank White coined the term "Overview Effect" to describe the mental shift in awareness that happens when someone views the Earth from orbit or the Moon. This experience profoundly affects the way human space explorers perceive the world and everything in it. It changes their perceptions of themselves, our planet, and our understanding of the future. They become very aware that we live on a planet that is like a natural spaceship moving rapidly through the universe. As the visionary Buckminster Fuller said, all people are the crew of "Spaceship Earth."

Back in the early 2000s, Interorbital Systems was working on a different idea for a spaceship. In 2002, they asked me to be their pilot. That sounded really exciting! Of course, I said yes. I went to California to see them test a small model of their rocket. It roared, and fiery exhaust shot out. I thought this was going to be my big chance. I wouldn't just be a passenger. I would actually fly the spaceship. Two years went by, and they stopped working on their rocket. I never got to fly their spaceship. I was disappointed again, but all I could do was throw it a fish.

In 2004, I went to California to watch another developer test a spaceship. This company had already built one. A funny-looking airplane with two bodies hooked together by a shared wing carried the spaceship high into the sky. Then the spaceship unhooked from the airplane, and its pilot started its rocket engine. It shot up to 62 miles above the Earth. It crossed into the edge of space! This company, Scaled Composites, actually built a private spacecraft that worked!

A few years later, I heard that a company called Virgin Galactic had hired Scaled Composites to build a bigger version of its little spaceship. This one would be able to carry six passengers on a suborbital spaceflight along with a pilot and a co-pilot. Some people came to visit me and asked me if I wanted to buy a ticket for a ride. Would I?

The ticket was very expensive, but this looked like my best chance ever to make my dream come true and fly into space. I bought the ticket. That was in 2010. The people at Virgin Galactic thought they would start flying passengers in two or three years. I was really excited this time!

It's harder to design a spaceship than most people realize, and after eleven years, I was still waiting. But 2021 would be the year when commercial spaceflight actually took flight!

Boy oh boy, did I get the surprise of my life in July 2021! Amazon founder Jeff Bezos invited me to be his honored guest aboard his space company's New Shepherd Rocket and go to space! When he told me that, my chin hit the floor, and I just grabbed him and hugged him tight! I really didn't think I'd ever get to go up, especially at the age of 82! Our date for flight was going to be July 20, 2021. How about them apples? On the 52nd anniversary of the Apollo 11 Moon Landing, I would get my chance to go to space!

Almost a week before my flight, Virgin Galactic got to spread its commercial spaceflight wings aboard Unity 22 and went more than 50 miles up into space on July 11, 2021. "I have dreamt of this moment since I was a kid, and honestly nothing could prepare you for the view of Earth from space," Sir Richard Branson said after landing. Watching him have success made me even more excited about my July 20th launch.

I'll never forget July 20, 2021, as it was the day I have waited for literally most of my life. Four of us were launched skyward on the New Shepard, a rocket developed by Mr. Bezos's firm, Blue Origin, from the West Texas desert. The spacecraft travelled at nearly three times the speed of sound, reaching a height of 66 miles above the Earth's surface.

I was the first one to unbuckle my seatbelt. I floated in three minutes of microgravity, looking out and seeing the Earth below! For me, as I told reporters, "It was EASY! I've been training for this my whole life." It was over entirely too quickly, but I am forever grateful to Jeff and Blue Origin for giving me the chance to make my dream a reality. Our capsule returned to Earth using parachutes ,and we landed softly in the desert. Our trip may have lasted little more than 10 minutes, but it fulfilled 62 years of dreams. As I exited the vessel, I spread my arms wide in joy!

With Virgin Galactic's success on July 11, 2021 and Blue Origin's on July 20, 2021, commercial spaceflight just became infinitely more accessible for all people. For me, it wasn't about billionaires, but access to space for people just like you and me.

Maybe Virgin Galactic will give me a call and tell me it's time to fly on their spacecraft soon! My ticket is paid, and Sir Richard and his team are welcome to call me anytime!

But here is what is most striking to me, and I don't mean to gloat. (My mom would not smile on my gloating, but maybe she will forgive me just this once.) At age 82, I became the oldest female who has ever gone to space, older than John Glenn when he went at age 77.

John Glenn set a record at age 77 when flying aboard space shuttle Discovery in 1998. The reason I take such pride in that is that he is the very astronaut that toed the NASA party line and said, "Men go to war, men fly planes, and men go to space" at the congressional hearing where Jerrie Cobb and Janey Hart were lobbying hard for women to become astronauts. His testimony put an end to our dreams of going to space at that time. So, gloat I will (sorry Mr. Glenn)! I went to space, not for as long as I would have liked or even how I dreamt I would, but go I did! And I can't tell you how monumental that realization is!

Sometimes, things we hope for don't happen when we want them to or the way we want them to. But I have learned to keep hoping and keep trying. If a dream is important, it's worth working for and waiting for. If my dream of going to space can happen at age 82, your dreams can happen, too. I pray that you let my spaceflight sink in as proof that dreams do not have an expiration date as long as we keep believing that they do indeed (eventually) come true.

Supersonic Hypersonic Life!

HOLY AIRPLANES! This just might be the longest letter I have ever written! I'll close this letter remembering I was one SUPERSONIC girl having a HYPERSONIC experience in this life! I can say truly I am very proud of all that I have done, and I get up every morning ready to take on my next adventure!

Whether it was the way I was brought up or just my personal nature, I have always been a positive person. I have enjoyed every moment of my life. When things haven't worked out the way I would have liked, my philosophy has always been to get over it and move on. I haven't changed.

Because of my quest for spaceflight as well as my aviation career, I have been invited to speak at interesting places all over the world. One place that has become very special to me is right here in the United States. The Portal of the Folded Wings is a beautiful, dome-covered building with four arched entryways at the Valhalla Cemetery in Burbank, California. It is a shrine to "the honored dead of American Aviation," and the ashes of more than a dozen aviation pioneers are interred under the floor of the structure.

In 2007, a 21-foot-long replica of a space shuttle was installed in front of the portal as a memorial to the astronauts who died in the Challenger and Columbia disasters. It was an honor for me to speak at the dedication of that memorial.

Bobbi Trout is one of the aviation pioneers whose ashes are buried in the portal. She set several aviation records back in the 1920s and 1930s. In later years, she became a dear friend and mentor to me. She died in 2003 at the age of 97. I have reserved a space for my ashes to be buried next to Bobbi's when it is my time to go.

I don't get emotional about passing from this life. I have faith that I will join my dear mother, my father, and my many friends who have gone before me when it is my turn to go. I have had a wonderful life filled with amazing experiences.

I have been preparing for my flight into space since 1960. Striving for that goal has already made my life more interesting and more exciting than it would have been otherwise. Because of that goal, my fascination with aviation, and my travels and hobbies, I have made many great friends.

Many of you may have read that on the same day that Blue Origin launched me and my other three crewmates aboard its suborbital mission using the New Shepard vehicle, the FAA announced a major change to its Commercial Space Astronaut Wings Program, which launched in 2004. Previously, to be eligible to earn the wings, commercial launch crew members had to both meet specific requirements for flight crew qualifications and training and fly above a 50-mile (80 km) altitude on an FAA-licensed or permitted vehicle.

Now with the new change, those who fly on commercial space missions must also have "demonstrated activities during flight that were essential to public safety, or contributed to human space flight safety." However, the FAA added that it can award "honorary" commercial space astronaut wings "to individuals who demonstrated extraordinary contribution or beneficial service to the commercial human spaceflight industry" without having to satisfy all eligibility requirements.

Well, fiddlesticks and throw it a fish is all I can say. The truth is I went up above 62 miles or 100 km, what is known as the Kármán line. That is the international definition of the edge of space. As of

December 10, 2021, I was awarded my FAA Astronaut wings, and I will always treasure my Blue Origin Astronaut pin. I am proud of both of these sets of 'wings', but nothing is greater than my own satisfaction at realizing my dream of being an astronaut and going to space.

Just remember this: if anyone ever tells you that you won't, can't, or shouldn't just because you're a girl (or different or just WHO YOU ARE)... you must prove them wrong, change their minds, and that's how you will change the world. AND ANOTHER THING...the only thing anyone ever needs to compete in a man's world is ABILITY!

Please don't let stress or fear into your life. You will lose faith in yourself if you let fear creep in. If you want to become skilled, competent, and professional, you need to be wise and know where you want to be in five or ten years.

And now I invite you to write a letter to your GENIUS self and imagine all that you will create, invent, innovate, and make known! Knowledge is the power that gives us wings to soar! Consider me your cheerleading co-pilot, always wishing you BLUE SKIES and TAIL WINDS! Take flight, my dear hearts! SOAR and dare to go higher and faster in your life!

This kid has no regrets. God bless you all.

Love,
Wally

Letter to My Genius Self

The Women of Mercury 13

This tribute patch celebrates the suborbital spaceflight of Wally Funk as the culmination of all of Mercury 13's space dreams realized. The patch was designed by Tim Gagnon, who has designed many space mission patches, see his work at kscartist.com. You can purchase this limited edition patch at janetsplanet.com.

This book has been about one of the Mercury 13, Wally Funk, with a couple of others mentioned briefly. Here is a summary of the other twelve members of the group and what they did after the program ended:

Jerrie Cobb was in many ways a leader of the group, much to the consternation of Jackie Cochran, who helped Dr. Lovelace organize the program and provided much of the financial support for it. After her efforts failed to keep the Women in Space program alive, Cobb spent most of her life in South America flying supplies to communities of indigenous people in the Amazon jungle. She died in 2019.

Myrtle "K" Cagle married a former flying student in 1960. She wore a wedding gown made of parachutes. She later became licensed as an airframe and power plant airplane mechanic and worked at Robbins Air Force Base in Georgia. Once, she was invited to visit Eglin Air Force Base in Florida by an Air Force general she interviewed for a newspaper column she was writing. On that 1953 visit, she was allowed to fly a T-33 jet airplane—a rare opportunity for a woman. She died in 2019.

Jan Dietrich had been a chief pilot for two flight schools, a test pilot for multi-engine aircraft for Cessna, and a pilot examiner for the FAA prior to her Lovelace testing. Later, during the Vietnam War, she worked for World Airways, a military contractor, flying regularly between its base in Oakland and the war zone. She stopped flying after the 1974 death of her twin sister, Marion. Jan died in 2008.

Marion Dietrich, Jan's twin sister, was a newspaper reporter as well as a commercial transport pilot who flew charter and ferry flights. After the Lovelace testing, the Dietrichs became allies of Jackie Cochran in opposing the Mercury 13 leadership of Jerrie Cobb. Marion died of cancer.

Sarah Gorelick (later Ratley) had a degree in mathematics and had worked for AT&T as an engineer. In later years, she became a certified public accountant and worked for the IRS. Her flying was personal and recreational. She died in 2020.

Jane "Janey" Hart was a helicopter pilot as well as an airplane pilot. She sometimes flew her husband, Senator Philip Hart, to speaking engagements when he was campaigning. She developed a friendship with feminist Betty Friedan and was a founding member of the National Organization for Women (NOW). During the administration of President Lyndon Johnson, Hart chaired the Women's Advisory Committee on Aviation for the FAA. She died in 2015.

Jean Hixson was a member of the Women Airforce Service Pilots (WASPs) during World War II, flying various types of non-combat missions including delivering aircraft to war zones. After the Lovelace testing, she joined the Air Force Reserves and worked on research projects involving space navigation and movement in reduced gravity during the Apollo era and beyond. She retired from the Air Force Reserves as a full colonel in 1982 and died in 1984.

Rhea Hurrle (later Woltman), a charter pilot, was one of only three of the Mercury 13 to take another type of astronaut qualification test, namely the isolation tank test that Cobb and Funk both took. Afterward, she helped with instruction at the Air Force Academy in Colorado. In 1972, she married and, without regret, stopped flying at the request of her new husband. She became a professional parliamentarian. She died in 2020.

Irene Leverton worked for a flight school that also flew Hollywood celebrities on air taxi flights. She took unauthorized time off for the abruptly cancelled Pensacola tests, and when she went back to work found her duties had been reduced to instructing beginning students. She later became an FAA certificated Airline Transport Pilot and served as a check pilot for a Civil Air Patrol squadron in Arizona. She died in 2017.

Jerri Sloan (later Truhill) co-owned a flying service that conducted equipment test flights for Texas Instruments and for the U.S. military. She served on the board of directors for the International Women's Air and Space Museum and became an active advocate for women's rights, particularly in aviation and aerospace. She died in 2013.

Bernice "B" Steadman owned her own aviation business, including an air taxi service, when she took part in the Lovelace tests. Later, she served as president of the Ninety-Nines and was a co-founder of the International Women's Air and Space Museum in Ohio. After suffering a brain injury in the 1970s, she stopped flying but continued to speak about careers in aviation and space. She died in 2015.

Gene Nora Stumbough (later Jessen) was teaching at Oklahoma State University when she applied for the Lovelace tests. Because the Pensacola tests would take place after the next semester started, she quit her job. Afterward, she found work as a flight instructor before becoming a sales demonstration pilot for Beechcraft airplanes. She later served as president of the Ninety-Nines and helped found the Ninety-Nines Museum of Women Pilots. She and Wally are currently the only living Mercury 13 women remaining.

174

Other Books about Women Pilots

Amelia: My First Amelia Earhart (Little People, Big Dreams)
Written by: Isabel Sanchez Vegara

Daredevil: The Daring Life of Betty Skelton
Written by: Meghan McCarthy

I Am Amelia Earhart
Written by: Brad Meltzer

Brave Harriet: The First Woman to Fly the English Channel
Written by: Marissa Moss

Aim for the Skies: Jerrie Mock and Joan Merriam Smith's Race to Complete Amelia Earhart's Quest
Written by: Aimee Bissonette

Fearless Flyer: Ruth Law and Her Flying Machine
Written by: Heather Lang

The Fearless Flights of Hazel Ying Lee
Written by: Julie Leung

Me and the Sky: Captain Beverley Bass, Pioneering Pilot
Written by: Beverley Bass, Cynthia Williams

Amelia And Eleanor Go For A Ride
Written by: Pam Munoz Ryan

Fly High! The Story Of Bessie Coleman
Written by: Louise Borden, Mary Kay Kroeger

Wood, Wire, Wings: Emma Lilian Todd Invents an Airplane
Written by: Kirsten W. Larson

Lighter Than Air: Sophie Blanchard, the First Woman Pilot
Written by: Matthew Clark Smith

Skyward: The Story of Female Pilots in WWII
Written by: Sally Deng

Amelia Lost: The Life and Disappearance of Amelia Earhart
Written by: Candace Fleming

Nerves of Steel: Young Readers Edition
The Incredible True Story of How One Woman Followed Her
Dreams, Stayed True to Herself, and Saved 148 Lives
Written by: Captain Tammie Jo Shults, Erin Healy

Born to Fly: The First Women's Air Race Across America
Written by: Steve Sheinkin

The Jerrie Mock Story: The First Woman to Fly Solo Around the World
Written by: Nancy Roe Pimm

Fly Girls Young Readers Edition: How Five Daring Women Defied
All Odds and Made Aviation History
Written by: Keith O'Brien

Yankee Doodle Gals: Women Pilots of World War II
Written by: Amy Nathan

Fly Girls: The Daring American Women Pilots Who Helped Win WWII
Written by: P. O'Connell Pearson

Women Aviators: 26 Stories of Pioneer Flights, Daring Missions, and Record-Setting Journeys
Written by: Karen Bush Gibson

Among the Red Stars
Written by: Gwen C. Katz

Seized by the Sun: The Life and Disappearance of World War II Pilot Gertrude Tompkins
Written by: James W. Ure

A Thousand Sisters: The Heroic Airwomen of the Soviet Union in World War II
Written by: Elizabeth Wein

A WASP Among Eagles: A Woman Military Test Pilot in World War II
Written by: Ann B. Carl

The Women with Silver Wings: The Inspiring True Story of the Women Airforce Service Pilots of World War II
Written by: Katherine Sharp Landdeck

Fighting For Space: Two Pilots and Their Historic Battle for Female Spaceflight
Written by: Amy Shira Teitel

Aviation Glossary

Absolute Altitude – The vertical distance between the aircraft and ground level.

Absolute Ceiling – The highest altitude an aircraft can fly at maximum throttle while maintaining level height and constant airspeed.

Adverse yaw – Occurs when the plane's nose turns away from the direction of turn.

Aileron – The movable, hinged flight control surfaces that are used in pairs with opposite motions to control the roll of an aircraft.

Airfoil – The cross-sectional shape of a wing, blade, turbine, or rotor that produces lift.

Air Speed Indicator (ASI) – A pitot-static flight instrument that indicates airspeed of an aircraft through an air mass in miles per hour, knots, or both.

Altimeter – An instrument that measures an object's altitude above a fixed surface.

Altitude Indicator – An instrument that indicates aircraft orientation relative to earth's horizon.

Angle of Attack – The angle between a reference line on an airfoil and the direction of the oncoming air.

Annual Inspection – A required aircraft inspection every 12 calendar months.

Approach – The phase of flight when the pilot intends to land on the runway.

Apron – The paved area at an airport where aircraft park, fuel, load, and unload.

ATC – *Air Traffic Control* – A ground-based service that ensures safety of air traffic by directing aircraft in the area during take-off, landing, and while flying in the designated airspace.

Avionics Master Switch – A single switch that controls the electrical power for an aircraft's electronic communication and navigation instruments.

Baseline – The minimum or starting point used for comparison.

Calibrated Airspeed – The indicated airspeed corrected for position and instrument error.

Camber – The convexity of curve on an aircraft wing.

CAVU – *Ceiling and Visibility Unlimited* – Describes ideal flying conditions with visibility of 10 or more miles and ceiling of at least 10,000 feet.

Cargo – Goods carried on an aircraft.

Ceiling – The height of the lowest cloud layer or obscuring phenomena that is reported as "broken", "overcast", or "obscuration", and not classified as "thin" or "partial."

Center of Gravity (CG) – The longitudinal and lateral point over which the aircraft would balance.

Clearance – The authorization provided by air traffic control for aircraft to proceed with a particular action in controlled airspace, which is designed to prevent aircraft collisions.

Climb – The act of increasing aircraft altitude, typically to a designated level.

CofA – Certificate of Airworthiness.

Contrail – A streak of condensed water vapor in the air due to the heat produced by aircraft engines at high altitudes.

Controlled Airspace – Designated airspace within which Air Traffic Control provides aircraft movement instructions and regulations.

Crosswind – Wind that is blowing perpendicular to the aircraft course.

Descent – The act of decreasing aircraft altitude, typically to a designated level.

Distress – An internationally-recognized signal for danger and need for immediate assistance.

Drag – A parallel and opposing force to an aircraft's motion through the air.

Elevator – Horizontal surfaces that control aircraft pitch and are typically hinged to the stabilizer.

Empennage – Another phrase for the tail of an aircraft, which provides stability during flight.

ETA – *Estimated Time of Arrival* – The time you will arrive at a destination, based on the local time.

FAA – *Federal Aviation Administration* – The governing body of civil aviation in the United States.

Feathering – The act of adjusting variable pitch propellers so that the blades are in line with airflow and don't create air resistance.

Final Approach – A flight path running in the direction of the runway intended for landing that ends with a landing.

Firewall – A fire-resistant bulkhead that is situated between the engine and other aircraft areas.

Flaps – Flaps are a kind of high-lift device used to increase the lift of an aircraft wing at a given airspeed. Flat devices, typically located on the edges of a an aircraft wing, that control lift at specific speeds.

Flight Deck – An area at the front of airplane where the pilot and aircraft controls are situated – in other words, the cockpit.

Flight Plan – Formatted information provided by pilots or dispatchers regarding an upcoming flight, including details such as destination, path, timing, etc.

Fog – Fog is a thick cloud of tiny water droplets at or near Earth's surface that obscures visibility.

Fuselage – The central portion of an aircraft, which is intended to house the flight crew, passengers, and cargo.

Glass Cockpit – A term used to describe an aircraft that is fully equipped with electronic, digital flight instrument displays, instead of analog-style gauges.

"George" – Nickname given to the autopilot system.

Groundspeed – The horizontal speed of an aircraft relative to the surface below.

Hangar – A building made to hold aircraft for storing, maintenance, assembly, etc.

Horizontal Stabilizer – The horizontal stabilizer prevents up-and-down, or pitching, motion of the aircraft nose.

Hypoxia – A condition caused by low levels of oxygen that can lead to dizziness, disorientation, etc., posing extreme danger to pilots operating aircraft at high altitudes.

Instrument Flight Rules (IFR) – Regulations that define aircraft operations when pilots are not able to operate using visual references. 183

Instrument Meterological Conditions (IMC) – Weather conditions that describe a situation where pilots are not able to operate using visual references.

Joystick – The control column in the aircraft is often called a joystick. It is the main device that controls the aircraft and is typically mounted on the ceiling or floor if the aircraft has a joystick instead of a yoke.

Knot – A measurement of speed that takes into account nautical miles: 1 knot = 1 nautical mile per hour = 6076 feet per hour. 1 mph =1 mile per hour = 5280 feet per hour.

Lift – The force that directly opposes aircraft weight, generated primarily by the wings.

Load Factor (g) – The smooth airflow over an aircraft wing with minimized drag.

Longitudinal Axis – The directional that runs horizontally from the aircraft nose to tail.

Mach – The ratio of aircraft speed to the speed of sound through the medium where the aircraft is traveling.

Magnetic Compass – The directional orientation of an aircraft according to the geomagnetic field.

Magnetic North – Unlike the geographical north (North Pole), this point is the location indicated as North by where the compass points.

MSL – Mean Sea Level – Average level of the surface of one or more of Earth's bodies of water from which heights such as elevation may be measured.

OAT – Outside Air Temperature.

Overshoot – Landing aircraft beyond the runway.

Payload – The weight of the content carried in an aircraft, including passengers, pilots, cargo, etc.

Pilot in Command (PIC) – The designated individual that is responsible for safe aircraft operations during flight.

Pitch – The movement of an aircraft, characterized by the nose and tail rising and falling.

Pitot Tube – A small device located on the front outside edge of an airfoil, used to measure air pressure.

Primary Flight Display (PFD) – The main screen used by pilots in aircraft containing an electronic flight instrument system.

Propeller – A piece of aircraft equipment that contains rotating blades, creating engine thrust.

Roll – Aircraft rotation along the longitudinal axis, which runs from the nose to tail.

Rudder – An aircraft surface used to control the yaw movement.

Runway (RWY) – A "defined rectangular area on a land aerodrome prepared for the landing and takeoff of aircraft."

Short Field – A runway that is shorter in length and requires aircraft to minimize the amount of runway used when taking off or landing.

Sideslip – An aircraft movement that typically aligns with the lateral force of the wind and results in a sideways flow.

Skid – The sliding and outward pivoting movement of the aircraft that occurs as a result of a shallow turn.

Slip – The sliding and inward pivoting movement of the aircraft that occurs as a result of a steep turn.

Soft Field – A runway that is not paved and made of elements such as dirt or grass.

Squawk – A four-digit code given to an aircraft by ATC to allow for simple identification of an aircraft in a given region.

Stability – Aircraft are subject to static, dynamic, longitudinal, lateral, and directional stability that impact flying conditions.

Stall – The condition that occurs as a result of an aircraft exceeding its angle of attack and therefore experiencing decreased lift.

Tail – The rear aircraft structure that provides aerodynamic stability.

Tarmac – The paved area at an airport where aircraft park, fuel, load, and unload.

Throttle – A device that controls the amount of power outputted by the engine.

Thrust – A force which opposes aircraft drag and is created by the engines to propel the aircraft forward.

Torque – A force that is intended to produce rotation.

Touch-and-Go – An aircraft maneuver used to practice landing techniques by simply landing on the runway and taking off once more without coming to a full stop.

Transponder – An electronic device on airplanes that generate an output code, which is used for ATC identification purposes.

Turbulence – A sudden violent shift in air flow caused by irregular atmospheric motion.

TWR – Tower.

Useful Load – The weight of the items that can be taken out of the aircraft, including fuel, passengers, cargo, pilots, etc.

Visual Flight Rules (VFR) – Regulations that define aircraft operations when pilots are able to operate using visual references.

Wind Shear – An abrupt change in horizontal or vertical wind direction.

Wx – Weather.

XC – Cross-country.

Yaw – The movement of an aircraft, characterized by the nose moving side-to-side.

Yoke – The aircraft control devices used by pilot for changes in attitude, as well as pitch and roll movement.

Zulu Time – A term synonymous with UTC (Universal Coordinated Time), which is the same as Greenwich Mean Time. Pilots file all flight plans in Zulu Time.

Female Firsts in Aviation

(This list is not exhaustive; we are sure there are many more female firsts in aviation.)

Aida de Acosta (1884–1962), first woman to fly a powered aircraft alone.

Pancho Barnes, granddaughter of balloonist Thaddeus Lowe; founded the Women's Air Reserve and the Associated Motion Picture Pilots, and became the "mother of the Air Force"

Ann Baumgartner (1918–2008), test pilot; first American woman to fly a U.S. Army Air Forces jet aircraft (a Bell YP-59A jet fighter). Jill E. Brown (born 1950), first African American female pilot for a major US carrier

Willa Brown (1906–1992), first black woman to hold both a commercial and private license in the US; founded the National Negro Airmen Association of America; first black female to be an officer in the Civil Air Patrol.

Mildred Mary Bruce (1895–1990), first woman to fly around the world alone.

Katherine Cheung, first Asian-American woman to get a pilot's license, in 1932.

Jerrie Cobb (1931-2019), first woman to fly in the Paris Air Show and to be tested as an astronaut.

Jacqueline Cochran (1908–1980), first woman to fly faster than the speed of sound.

Bessie Coleman, first African-American woman pilot and first Native American to earn her pilot's license, in France in 1921.

Eileen Collins, former test pilot and NASA astronaut; first female pilot and first female commander of a space shuttle.

Jessica Cox, world's first armless licensed pilot.

Amelia Earhart (1897–1937), first woman to fly solo across the Atlantic.

Wally Funk, one of the Mercury 13; first female air safety inspector at the FAA and first female accident investigator for the NTSB

Shawna Rochelle Kimbrell, first African American female fighter pilot in U.S. Air Force.

Raymonde de Laroche, first woman in the world to get an airplane pilot's license, in 1910

Hazel Ying Lee, Chinese-American pilot who flew for the U.S. Army Air Forces during World War II.

Elsie MacGill, world's first female aircraft designer, known as "Queen of the Hurricanes."

Pamela Melroy, former NASA astronaut who served as pilot and commander on space shuttle missions

Jerrie Mock, first woman to fly solo around the world.

Ruth Nichols (1901–1960), set many aviation records and started the first air ambulance service in the US.

Phoebe Omlie, first woman to receive an airplane mechanic's license; first licensed woman transport pilot.

Harriet Quimby (1875–1912), first woman to get a U.S. pilot's license and fly across the English Channel

Ola Mildred Rexroat, only Native American woman to serve in the Women Air Force Service Pilots (WASPs)

Bonnie Tiburzi, first female pilot for American Airlines and the first female pilot for a major American commercial airline.

Bobbi Trout (1906–2003), set endurance records and was the first woman to fly all night.

Pilot Jargon

"Let's kick the tires and light the fires" is the military phrase that signals a plane is just about ready for takeoff. Once the crew completes the pre-flight gear inspection, it's time to ignite the engine and take to the sky.

"Feet wet" This phrase alerts air traffic controllers when a military aircraft, (usually a Navy carrier pilot), is flying over water. Once a flight has crossed the shore and resumes flying over land, they'll call in to air traffic control that their "feet dry."

"It's 17:00 Zulu time" Since pilots can pass through multiple time zones in one trip and must communicate with air traffic controllers from around the world, aviators follow "Zulu time," or Greenwich Mean Time (GMT), the universal time zone of the skies. GMT is the time kept by the Royal Observatory in Greenwich, London. So, if it's 2 a.m. in London for example, it'll be 02:00 "Zulu time" for every pilot in the air.

"George is flying the plane now" There's a "George" on nearly every commercial aircraft, but he's not a crew member. "George" is a nickname for a plane's autopilot system that follows a programmed set of points to the flight's destination, taking into consideration changes in turbulence and altitude.

"We're flying through an air pocket" Turbulence-averse flyers, beware: "air pocket" is just another word for the winds that jostle a plane from different directions. The term "air pocket" causes less panic than "turbulence" among passengers.

"Tree," "fife" and "niner" Aviators often speak "pilot English" to avoid miscommunications over radio transmission. "Tree" for instance, means three, "fife" is the number five and "niner" means nine. The variations stemmed from a desire to avoid confusion between similar-sounding numbers.

"Pan-Pan" Airline passengers likely won't ever hear their pilot use this term, which is reserved for communication with air traffic controllers. When pilots notice something unusual with their aircraft that stops short of an immediate emergency, they use "pan-pan," a signal of urgency and attention. If one of a multi-engine aircraft's engines has failed, for example, pilots might say "pan-pan" to get controllers' attention and request an emergency landing.

Resources

Air Race Classic: Women's air racing started in 1929 with the Women's Air Derby. Twenty pilots raced from Santa Monica, CA to Cleveland, OH, site of the National Air Races. Racing continued through the 30s and was renewed again after WWII when the All Women's Transcontinental Air Race (AWTAR), better known as the Powder Puff Derby, came into being in 1947. The AWTAR held its 30th, final, and commemorative flight in 1977. When the AWTAR was discontinued, the Air Race Classic (ARC) stepped in to continue the tradition of transcontinental speed competition for women pilots and staged its premier race.
https://www.airraceclassic.org

All-American Girls Professional Baseball League: The AAGPBL Player's Association is a non-profit organization dedicated to preserving the History of the AAGPBL and supporting women and girls all across our country who deserve the opportunity to play "Hardball."
https://www.aagpbl.org

Association for Women in Aviation Maintenance: AWAM is a nonprofit organization formed for the purpose of championing women's professional growth and enrichment in aviation maintenance by providing opportunities for sharing information and networking, education, fostering a sense of community, and increasing public awareness of women in the industry.
https://www.awam.org

Fédération Aéronautique Internationale: The Fédération Aéronautique Internationale, FAI, the World Air Sports Federation, was founded in 1905. It is a non-governmental and non-profit making international organization with the basic aim of furthering aeronautical and astronautical activities worldwide, ratifying world and continental records and coordinating the organization of international competitions. It is recognized by the International Olympic Committee (IOC).
https://www.fai.org

International Forest of Friendship: The International Forest of Friendship is a living, growing memorial to the world history of aviation and aerospace. The Forest was a gift to America on her 200th birthday in 1976 from the City of Atchison, Kansas (the birthplace of Amelia Earhart); The Ninety-Nines (International Organization of Women Pilots), and the Kansas State University, Kansas Forest Service.
https://ifof.org

National Intercollegiate Flying Association: The National Intercollegiate Flying Association (NIFA) was formed for the purposes of developing and advancing aviation education; to promote, encourage and foster safety in aviation; to promote and foster communications and cooperation between aviation students, educators, educational institutions and the aviation industry; and to provide an arena for collegiate aviation competition.
https://nifa.aero

Ninety-Nines: The Ninety-Nines, Inc., is an international organization of licensed women pilots from 44 countries.
https://www.ninety-nines.org

Single Action Shooting Society: The Single Action Shooting Society is an international organization created to preserve and promote the sport of Cowboy Action Shooting™. SASS endorses regional matches conducted by affiliated clubs, stages END of TRAIL The World Championship of Cowboy Action Shooting, promulgates rules and procedures to ensure safety and consistency in Cowboy Action Shooting matches, and seeks to protect its members' 2nd Amendment rights.
https://sassnet.com

Women in Aviation International: Women in Aviation International (WAI) is a nonprofit organization dedicated to the encouragement and advancement of women in all aviation career fields and interests.
https://www.wai.org

Women in Military Service to America Memorial: The Women In Military Service For America Memorial, at the Ceremonial Entrance to Arlington National Cemetery, is the only major national memorial honoring all women who have defended America throughout history. Their patriotism and bravery are a part of our nation's heritage and are now recognized. *https://www.womensmemorial.org*

Zonta International: Zonta International is a leading global organization of professionals empowering women worldwide through service and advocacy. *https://www.zonta.org*

About Janet Ivey-Duensing

Janet Ivey

- *Creator and CEO of Janet's Planet, Inc.*
- *President of Explore Mars (2019-2022)*
- *Citizen Astronaut Candidate for Space For Humanity*
- *NASA JPL Solar System Ambasador*
- *Award-winning Science Educator*
- *12 Regional Emmy Awards*
- *5 Gracie Awards*
- *STEM-FLORIDA Award for Exploring Microgravity, documentary geared to K-12 students*
- *Board of Governors for the National Space Society*
- *2 Tedx Talks, AWE Inspired Science Camp; How To Inhabit Your Very Own*
- *Planet #PlanetYou*

Janet Ivey-Duensing, award winning children's TV host is the host Of Janet's Planet, a public television science series for children. A cheerful, energetic, creative voice for STEM education, Janet constantly seeks new opportunities to engage people in her love for science. Janet is an advocate, educator, communicator, and female role model of STEM/STEAM and is committed to sharing the joy of exploration and discovery with children around the globe. Janet's mission is to encourage science literacy globally and particularly to embody the role of female science mentor for the next generation of women in space and science. The mission for Janet and Janet's Planet is to encourage young people to stand in their inherent magnificence and to inspire future generations to use their innate intelligence and creativity to create a better future In addition to her other work, Janet Ivey-Duensing is writing a series of books called Unsung Genius / Letter to My Genius Self, which celebrates lesser-known scientists, especially women and other minorities. The first in the series was Mary Anning: Daring to Dig about the famed woman paleontologist. Written in cooperation with author Loretta Hall and aviation pioneer Wally Funk, this second book, Wally Funk: Higher Faster Longer, takes the series to the skies and beyond. Janet lives by a lake outside Nashville with her husband and her dogs.

You can find her at https://www.janetsplanet.com .

About Loretta Hall

Loretta Hall and Wally Funk

Loretta Hall has been intrigued with human spaceflight since her adolescent years. She followed the progress of the Mercury, Gemini, and Apollo missions and was thrilled to watch the first human steps on the Moon in 1969. The images on her black-and-white television screen were shadowy and almost ghostlike, but the accomplishment was clear.

Loretta shared this fascination with millions of people around the world, including Wally Funk. Wally is a visual person, and she even took snapshot photos of her television screen showing the first Moonwalkers.

Wally and Loretta didn't meet until nearly fifty years later, but they quickly became friends. By this time, Loretta had become a freelance writer and had written eight books, half of them about space exploration. Wally had decided it was time to record her life story in book form. The partnership was natural.

Another thing Loretta and Wally have in common is a love of New Mexico. In 1977, Loretta and her husband, Jerry Hall, moved to Albuquerque. They raised their three daughters there and put down deep roots. Wally was born and raised in northern New Mexico and has always regarded the state as her physical and emotional home.

Loretta is active in the writing and space communities. She has served as an elected officer for six years in New Mexico Press Women and was named 2016 Communicator of Achievement by the National Federation of Press Women. She is a subcommittee member and a Certified Space Ambassador for the National Space Society.

You can find out more about Wally and Loretta and contact them through their websites: *WallyFly.com* and *AuthorHall.com*.

About the Katie Grayson

Katie Grayson

Katie Grayson is an artist and illustrator from Nashville, Tennessee. The oldest of six children, she learned early to escape into her imagination, where she fell in love with dinosaurs, astronauts, sharks, and dragons. After studying art seriously for the past eight years, she is launching a career in commercial art with murals, logos, and artwork for books. She is also working on writing and illustrating a series of children's books that celebrate kids from diverse backgrounds in fantasy and science fiction environments.

You can find her at *katiegraysonart.com*.

CPSIA information can be obtained
at www.ICGtesting.com
Printed in the USA
JSHW050430190522
25885JS00003B/7